t

The Fisherman's Cottage

The Fisherman's Cottage

Our quest for good food, love, and a corkscrew

Bill Huebsch

Illustrations by Mark Hakomaki

Also by Bill Huebsch

How to Live Well & Do Good

How to Recognize Grace When You See It

How God Speaks to Us in Prayer

And many other titles, all found at Amazon.com

Bill Huebsch
The Fisherman's Cottage

Bill Huebsch lives in St Paul, Minnesota, USA
and Milverton, Somerset, England.
He is a writer, a gardener, a husband,
a university professor, and a corkscrew operator.
They love nothing more than to share a meal
with friends.

This is for Mark

First edition, August 2019
Published by Amazon.com.

Cover art from 123RF. Permission for use is on file.
Inside art and illustrations by Mark Hakomaki.
http://www.markhakomaki.com/

ISBN: 9781689006385

Acknowledgments

My thanks. There is no one to whom I owe more gratitude than Mark Hakomaki. He has illustrated this book, but he has also illustrated my life with romance, good food, and great adventures.

Our friends. I am deeply indebted to the many friends—over more than two decades now—who have accompanied us to St Ives for the Christmas holidays. The characters of Claire and Philip are drawn from you all! I have cleverly disguised any outstanding personality traits so that—in case you're one of those friends—you will never suspect I am speaking specifically of you. Yeah, right.

My leitmotif. Our experience of St Ives and of England as a whole would not be the same were it not for the genius of Kenneth Grahame and his beloved classic, *The Wind in the Willows*. The characters in that book have accompanied us annually, and I have shamelessly borrowed from this work to invite his lovely creatures into this telling of the story. The illustrations at the top of chapters 8, 15, and 18 are an adaptation of those done by Ernest H. Shepard for the original book. This work was published before January 1, 1924, and is in the public domain worldwide because the author died at least 100 years ago.

Contents

The Appetizer
With a toast to St Ives!

The tale I'm about to tell you is one that I'm hesitant to share. Down at the end of England, there lies a duchy called Cornwall and a village called St Ives. This is a place full of stories. They're stories set along a coast with azure-colored air and green hillsides populated with sheep and cattle. The people who live here are part of ancient stories wrapped up with tardy saints, tin miners, and hard-working fishermen. These are tales of unexpectedly outstanding cuisine shared with friendly people amid crackling pub fires. They're tales of a village—St Ives—that was discovered by a school of artists who have made an indelible contribution to how we see beauty—each one contributing from his or her own vision.

St Ives is smack in the middle of an English countryside bedecked with gorse and heather, hedgerows and fence lines. These ancient natural wonders that have stood their ground for hundreds of years and thousands of sheep. The roads lead westward and eventually come to rest at the cape where the Atlantic Ocean and the Celtic Sea meet. This coastal area is cut deep with clefts and fissures where the winds come up and blow the anxieties and tensions of modern life right out of you.

I'm hesitant to tell you about this place because I don't want you to find it; I'm afraid you might go there. When a lot of people go to a place, then sometimes it loses its spiritual charm. Like the guy who killed the goose that laid the golden egg, I don't want anyone killing my St Ives goose.

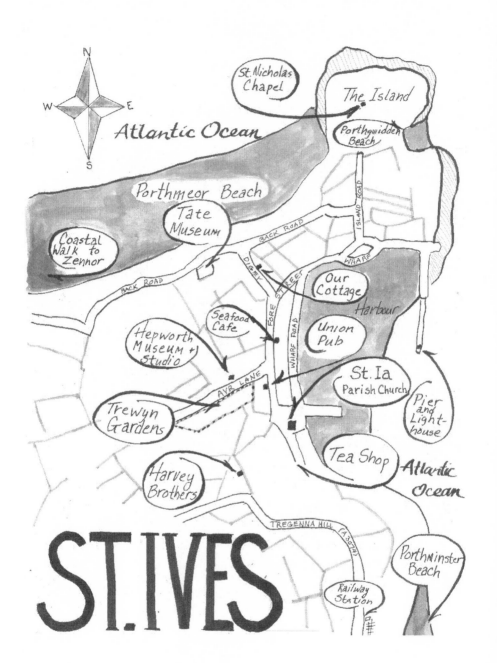

St. Nicholas Chapel

The Island

Atlantic Ocean

Porthgwidden Beach

Porthmeor Beach

Tate Museum

Coastal Walk to Zennor

BACK ROAD

ISLAND ROAD

WHARF

Our Cottage

Harbour

Seafood Cafe

BACK ROAD

DIGEY

FORE STREET

WHARF ROAD

Hepworth Museum + Studio

Union Pub

St. Ia Parish Church

Pier and Lighthouse

AYR LANE

Trewyn Gardens

Tea Shop

Atlantic Ocean

Harvey Brothers

TREGENNA HILL (A3074)

ST. IVES

Porthminster Beach

Railway Station

The Fisherman's Cottage

Chapter 1

Porthmeor Beach & Tate St Ives

"Are you ready to get a little mud on your shoes?" we asked our guests over breakfast. They looked down at their lightweight sneakers and back up at us. "How much mud?"

Philip and Claire had journeyed with us to St Ives, Cornwall, to celebrate the Christmas holidays. Even though they'd visited the British Isles often over the years, this was their first time here. We were down at the end of England, where the moors meet the sea. Mark and I had been making this our holiday home for many years. We were eager to revisit some of our old haunts and to share them with these friends. A favorite place of ours was the coastal pathway leading west out of St Ives. These footpaths crisscross and surround this Cornish peninsula. Mud? Oh yes, But Philip and Claire were good hikers, and we knew they'd love this hike. They were both Anglophiles, and we had promised them unforgettable views, pubs galore, and friendly sheep.

We had always found that every adventure is more pleasurable if you start with a good meal. The idea of traipsing out on an empty stomach left us, well, feeling empty. So, on this day, after our first night's sleep in the fisherman's cottage, we were diving into scones and jam with fruit, yogurt, and granola. Not a typical English breakfast but we thought it would fortify us for the day's adventures. Looking up now from his clotted cream and blackberry jam for a minute, Philip wiped his chin to ask more about the mud. December is a rainy month in Cornwall, which is saying a lot since every month is wet. A little rain had fallen overnight, so the prospect of getting a bit dirty seemed likely to him. "So, the mud," he said. "What kind of mud is this?"

"Well, to be honest, it's not all mud." Philip looked at me over his glasses, so I explained. "It's also partly sheep poop."

"Sheep poop?" Claire had a scowl on her face. "You guys are such farmer types. Why is there always poop around?" On their last visit to our farm in Minnesota, Claire had managed to step into a rather large pile of the stuff in our pasture. We had warned her not to show up in open-toed shoes, but did she listen?

"How do you think animals live? They don't have bathrooms," we told her.

"I know that. It's just, I don't know. Shouldn't someone go around picking it all up or something?"

I looked at Philip, asking with my eyes if he could do anything with her. "Don't worry, honey" he told her. "We'll tread carefully."

St Ives is a fishing village on the north coast of the southwest tip of Cornwall, a four or five-hour drive from London. It is, as I said, down at the end of England. It's across the peninsula from Penzance and, of course, their pirates are famous. In the summer, this is a beach town, filled with sun lovers and surfers. But in the winter, the town belongs to the local folks and a handful of visitors who come here for Christmas. Most of the shops and restaurants stay open all winter, or at least through the New Year holiday, so with smaller crowds and grateful merchants it's an easy place to spend the holidays.

"Oh," we told them, "a little mud is good. It keeps you grounded." And off we went, out the doorway of our fisherman's cottage, down the narrow stone stair, and out onto "the Digey." In St Ives, the Digey (pronounced dye-jhee) is a well-known passageway between Fore Street and the St Ives Harbor on one side and Porthmeor Beach on the other. It's narrow and cobblestoned, barely wide enough for a very small car to pass.

We turned right and headed down toward the beach where surfers were bobbing in the chilly water waiting for their big wave. They were wearing wetsuits to keep them warm in the meantime. The tide was coming in that morning, so the water's edge was still thirty yards or more from the granite and stone seawall on which we stood. Surfers here favor a 'low going high' tide—when it's on the rise. This rising tide helps create the beloved "tidal push" as the waves come crashing toward the shore. It's this surge for which the surfers were waiting as they paddled along in the cold water.

"Looks chilly to me," Philip said, pulling up his scarf against the morning sea breeze. None of us disagreed. For Claire and Philip, this was their first glimpse of the sea in St Ives. Huge clouds stood on the horizon to the north. But the sky above us was mostly clear and the morning sun came in from the east to our right. It splashed across the beach. The color of the seawater here is so blue that even Mark—who is an artist and painter and who works with colors every day on his palette—has a hard time describing it. It's azure—or is it turquoise? In this bright sun, it was spectacular. Many people who see this for the first time are entranced by it.

We were. Mark and I made our first trip here nearly twenty years earlier than this visit with Claire and Philip. We keep coming back. The first time we turned the corner from the Digey onto the flats along this seawall was unforgettable. It quickly became one of our most beloved places. The first moments that we spent standing here two decades earlier, gazing out across this beach—we'll never forget them. No photo of this sea could ever capture its essence and power. No written description can do it justice.

The four of us turned left at the seawall and followed the Digey Flats, pausing to watch the scene unfolding in front of us. The beach was full of people: dog walkers, children, lovers, and one or two people who were brave enough to go into the water in December. Beach watching was mesmerizing somehow, and we all four stood there in silence, entranced by the movement of people in front of us. The beach was at least a quarter-mile long; it wasn't possible to see both ends of it. We were each watching different stories unfold in front of us on this expanse: a family with two dogs and three kids; a young couple walking arm in arm; an old gentleman in a long coat out on a solitary stroll. If the water is blue, the color of the air in the morning light was a stunning blue-green as the waves produced a light mist above them. Not even Franco Zeffirelli could have orchestrated this complex scene. It was natural and spontaneous, and the stage belonged to everyone.

After a while, we turned and continued our walk, passing in front of Tate St Ives, its sizeable sea-grey rotunda to our left. St Ives had long been home to the stunning Barbara Hepworth gardens and museum. In 1980 the Tate started to manage the Hepworth collections and to expand its support of local arts, especially artists closely linked with Henry Moore. (Moore and Hepworth had studied together at the Leeds School of Art back in the day.) In 1988, the Tate decided to open a gallery here to feature the art of St Ives; and there is a lot of art here to show. The directors at the Tate purchased a former gasworks and commissioned architects Eldred Evans and Philip Shalev who created a design for the gallery following a style similar to that of the old gas plant. The new building overlooks Porthmeor Beach, and it includes the massive, grey rotunda at the center of the gallery at which we suddenly realized we were silently staring.

"Wow," Claire said after a moment, almost breathlessly, "Didn't expect to find that here." The Tate first opened its doors in Britain in 1897. At that time, there was just one site, and everything on display was British. It's a much more significant organization today with four locations, and seventy-thousand (yes, *seventy* thousand!) works from all around the world. Its namesake is Henry

Tate who made his fortunes as a sugar refiner. He offered his collection to the country in 1889—along with enough money to care for it—and the rest is history.

We made a note that visiting the Tate would be one of our goals for the week, but we continued to walk along the seawall, past the Beach Café. We could smell their fresh morning coffee and pastries, and we were tempted to stop even though we had just finished breakfast an hour before. The great thing about being on holiday is that you can stop anytime and anywhere you want. How lovely to have so little to do that it doesn't really matter whether or not you do it. I have this place I go to near our home in St Paul where I can sit and, well, that's it. I just sit. I'm not speaking or even rehearsing what smart thing I might say later. I'm not working or reading. I'm certainly not looking at my so-called smartphone. I'm just sitting. I am, as Gilles Deleuze aptly put it in *Negotiations,* doing nothing whatsoever.

It takes a lot of nerve to avoid the temptation to do something more meaningful. We're often in the habit of "keeping our shoulders to the wheel" in life. We're so accustomed to working that we often feel guilty when we stop. A lot of people "work their way through their holidays," keeping to a tight schedule and making sure they see and do everything while staying in close touch with their entire family and most of their friends via various electronic gadgets.

On one of our first visits to Paris many years ago, I remember that Mark and I would go out every morning, marching along with our guidebooks and plans for the day. We were purposeful. But we kept seeing all these Parisians who were just sitting in cafes, smoking and sipping on espressos or Pastis. They were all just sitting there, chatting with each other in that fashionable *sotto voce*. They looked like they were having a great time doing basically nothing. Having a great time hadn't occurred to us; we were busy *working* on having fun. On that trip, we were staying in the neighborhood of cafes where the Rue Dauphine meets the Rue de Buci. There are lots of galleries and shops in this part of the Saint Germain, especially on the Rue de Seine and the Rue Mazarine. We had a lot to get done! We had to keep moving.

It took us several years, but eventually, we learned how to *spend* the day doing nothing rather than *waste* it by working so hard. We finally figured out that we did not have to accomplish every damn thing we had on our list. These days we go to Paris primarily to spend time sitting in those cafes.

On this morning in St Ives, we had plans. We were heading for a hike along the Coast Path, westerly out of town toward Zennor. But that coffee did smell good. "Why not?" Philip said. "Let's stop. Is the Coast Path going to disappear? The mud can wait."

The South West Coast Path on which we were about to embark includes six-hundred-thirty miles of public footpaths along the Devon and Cornish coastlines. It's the longest national trail in England, and St Ives is smack in the middle of it. If you walk up to the seashore at pretty much any spot and turn either left or right, you're on the Coast Path. This coast, with its moors and hollows, has long captured the imaginations of moviemakers, television producers, writers, and artists. Doc Martin is set up the coast at Port Issac. Poldark is set pretty much everywhere in Cornwall. Even Sherlock Holmes gets into the act since he is said to have retired here after his illustrious career. He's somewhere up toward Devon raising bees.

One of the most famous writers who set her works here is Dame Rosamunde Pilcher. Her literary career lasted some fifty years during which she published more than twenty novels and many collections of short stories. These novels and the movies they spawned highlighted life, death, and love on this coast. And isn't that what writers and artists do? We often understand a place or an event through the eyes of those who tell its stories, whether on a page, in a song, or on a canvas. We hear people speak of "Dickens' London" as though he owned it, which, in a way, is correct. He owned its stories because he told them to us so well.

What artists and writers help us see goes beyond the surface of a place; they help us understand the deeper meaning, the interior light of an event or a situation. In each age, this takes a different form, and St Ives is an artists' community that reflects that. From realism to impressionism to modernism, each period gave us new insight, a new facet of St Ives, until we have what we do today. And yet, even this understanding will evolve as new artists and writers retell the stories again and again. Even the story about St Ives that Mark and I are telling Philip and Claire this week will be new when they see it through their own eyes. They'll discover this coastal hike, for example, in their own words and on their own terms. But first, the Café is waiting.

We ordered coffee and tea, along with a sweet pastry to fortify us for our hike. As we sat down, Claire asked about this place. "Oh my God," she started. "I can't believe where we are. We just drove in here yesterday afternoon and moved into our cottage. I had no idea I'd be sitting here today between this enormous beach with all these people roaming around on it and a *Tate* Museum. How long has this been here?"

A lot of people have never found this place we assured her. She wasn't the last person on earth to wander into this village. "The world is full of places like this which are off the beaten path," Philip told her. "The people who live here have "discovered" it, of course." I could feel Philip shift into his philosophical self. This could be a long cup of coffee. "Well, you know, the indigenous people of North America were there long before the place was "discovered" by Europeans," he started. But we were saved because at this point, the waiter brought our coffee and tea to the table. Claire looked her over, and I knew she was going to engage her. "So, are you a surfer?" Claire asked?

"Oh, God, no. I'm totally cack-handed. I'd drown. And besides, the water's too cold. I think they're all bloody nuts." And she marched off. She had snake tattoos on each arm and bright red hair.

"I think they're all bloody nuts," Claire repeated quietly after tattoo girl left the table, trying to imitate her accent. "I think they're all bloody nuts."

"Well, here's to those plucky surfers," we toasted with our coffee cups.

"And here's to this place," Philip added. Then he turned his chair to see out the windows and look toward the water. From our perch on the porch of the café, we could see beneath us on the beach where a small group of would-be surfers was lined up in the local surfing school. They were getting their first surfing instructions, and they looked eager and fit. This surf school often includes pro surfers on its faculty and works right here in the middle of St Ives. You wouldn't think that surfing in December would be so popular, but the water is busy almost every day.

The surfing is all here at Porthmeor Beach, but the kayaking, stand-up paddling, and something called coasteering all happen across town at Porthminster Beach, which is also the harbor. Coasteering involves a wild combination of climbing across rocks, floating through sea gullies, exploring caves, and negotiating rock jumps. It's an adrenaline rush for anyone who tries it, but it's not a sport for the faint of heart, and probably not for us. We finished our coffee and decided to head safely out on *terra firma*.

"I think they're all bloody nuts," Claire was muttering as we left the Café.

Chapter 2

The Coast Path

We headed west, farther along the seawall. There we stepped off the streets and onto the footpath that took us past the St Ives Bowls Club. Lawn bowling, which is called *bocce* ball in Italy and *boules* in France, is still a popular sport in St Ives. This club was founded in 1908 and is still going strong. The annual bowling season ends in September, but there were half a dozen plucky, older gentlemen on the green today, neck scarves waving in the wind as they rolled the balls.

"Calling it a sport might be a bit much," Mark said, "I mean, it's totally possible to play this game while holding a pint of ale in one hand and the ball in the other."

"That's my kind of sport," Philip said. "Where do I sign up?"

The game is played by rolling balls across the lawn with enough finesse that they stop near a smaller ball called a jack which has also been put into play. The player whose balls are nearest—but not touching—the jack, scores. All this ball rolling happens on a bowling green like the one we were passing. It was a flat, grassy area, and it was clearly necessary to keep the grass mowed quite short. Before lawnmowers were available, they grazed sheep on the green to keep it mowed. What a great idea! We discussed this as we walked.

"Where did the sheep poop?" Claire wanted to know.

"What's with you and sheep poop?" I asked. "Good grief. But since you asked, I'll tell you. Sheep have involuntary sphincters, so they poop wherever and whenever the urge strikes."

"First of all, why do you know so much about the sphincters of sheep?"

"Doesn't everyone?" I shrugged.

Claire went on, "Oooh. I wouldn't wanna play ball in that stuff."

"But it's all fertilizer."

"Yuk."

We continued along the Coast Path and walked by a rocky outcropping called Man's Head Point, so named because, well, it looks like a man's head, I guess. It's on the west end of that large Porthmeor beach. We paused here and turned around, looking back at the granite houses in the village. The geology of Cornwall is the story of granite, we tell Philip. Claire's gone off to examine the flora along the pathway. Granite formed beneath the surface of the earth here over long centuries from magma which crystallized. Here in Cornwall, there's a lot of granite to be mined. Before masons learned to cut and shape it, though, they built with granite stones found scattered around on the moors.

"You mean, they just went out on the moors and picked up stones to build houses? And they found enough? That's remarkable," Philip said.

From our vantage point at Man's Head Point, we couldn't see the harbor because it's on the other side of town. But that harbor was far more critical than this beach to the history of St Ives. It was the home of a very productive fishing industry here. The fishing pier was built in 1770 by John Smeaton. The prosperity of this town came, not from tourists and surfers then but from pilchard, mackerel, and herring. Fishers long worked their boats and nets from that harbor. They lived in the surrounding neighborhoods which produced an enchanting part of town known locally as "the Downalong." This neighborhood is a maze of interlocking streets and tiny alleyways. The Digey on which we are spending our holiday is one of those small streets, and ours is one of those fisher family's cottages.

As we looked back toward the village, we could see the hillside cemetery which leaned toward the sea. Its neat rows of memorials were filled with sailors, fishers, and their families. Fishing and St Ives go together like, well, fish and chips.

In the 1800s, fishermen organized themselves into lodges. There was the Shore Shelter Lodge, for example, with sixteen members, or the Shamrock Lodge, which started out with just four members but grew to a dozen within a few years. These lodges provided a sort of fishing club so the men would not have to work alone. Members of a given lodge were always watching out for each other. A Fishermen's Co-op was also established to help families afford nets, boats, and equipment. St Ives was a fishing village, no doubt about that. Early settlers organized the town around its harbor, and the families depended on both the weather and the town lifeboat crew for safekeeping. When the weather or the shoals brought them trouble—and when the lifeboat crew got there too late—the family made a trip to this cemetery to bury their dead.

With the sea crashing onto the headlands behind us, we all understood the risks of heading out to make a living on lightweight fishing boats. The sea is vast and holds natural power over life and death. Those who make their living on it know its dangers well. Alfred, Lord Tennyson, the Victorian Poet Laureate of Great Britain, expressed this well in his poem "Crossing the Bar." When a sailor speaks of "crossing the bar," he refers to that final passage over the sand bar which one finds at the entrance to every harbor. Once crossed, the sailors are indeed out in that enormous and moody sea. The poet here is suggesting that in life, we also cross the bar into what he calls "the boundless deep." Hence this cemetery, filled with fishers and sailors. It's a stark reminder that life is precious but that death always lies justs across that bar for all of us.

Interestingly, Tennyson wrote that poem at the end of his life. He died only a few years later. He requested that this poem appear last in any collection of his works. The last two stanzas of the poem are beautiful:

> Twilight and evening bell,
> And after that, the dark!
> And may there be no sadness of farewell,
> When I embark;
>
> For though from out our bourne of Time and Place
> The flood may bear me far,
> I hope to see my Pilot face to face
> When I have crossed the bar.

.

As we stood there looking back at the village quietly for a minute, I shivered a little in my tweed jacket, tightened it up just a bit against the winds, and we headed farther down the path. It wasn't warm, but it wasn't cold either. December in St Ives is the month in which we see early flowers blooming, such as the gorse which was abundant here. Farmers are harvesting cauliflower and brussels sprouts during this month. Today's weather is dry, but December weather here is always "variable." We don't even bother to check local forecasts; they all predict "sunshine unless there is drizzle." We trudged onward. The path was wide enough to walk two abreast unless we met other walkers. Now and then a runner whizzed by, but mainly we were alone on the path. We were walking to the west and, before long, the town behind us disappeared, and our only view was of the headlands and the water.

Pretty soon, the Coast Path started to turn and wind, moving up and down along the sea. The bituminous surfacing came to an end and lo, there was the mud we had promised Philip and Claire. The path wasn't always easy to follow as it meandered. We hiked on toward Zennor, the next village west along this coast, but without any intention of actually getting that far. The path sometimes hugged the high headlands along the seashore, and at other times it led inland to pass around clefts in the rocks and hills. There are no trees here; none could survive the winds. Windy, open moors or coastal grasslands like these are covered in that gorse which Claire had noticed. It hugs the narrow footpath and fills in the hedgerows. Gorse is an evergreen with needle-like leaves; it's a member of the pea family. The bright yellow flowers of gorse along with purple heathers give the whole landscape a wild look.

We were the only people in sight now, and the terrain was getting more and more untamed. No more benches or paved pathways. In fact, the path itself was now almost impossible to make out. The beauty of this place was on full display that morning. The light was gorgeous as it highlighted the hills and produced shadows on their backsides. The sea was powerful as the tide was coming in, loud, splashy, and bright.

Along the way, we passed through ingenious gates that allowed humans to move through but kept the sheep and cattle on the other side. They're called "kissing gates" because the swinging gate merely "kisses" the gatepost without ever being attached to it. Gate makers build these by setting a series of posts in a V-shaped pattern. They have a hinged gate trapped between the open points of the V. The gate swings between these points, and when stopped at either side of the enclosure, there is no opening to pass through. A human can easily push the gate to one side, step to the other, and push the gate back, passing through. But no animal can figure this out.

Where a kissing gate wouldn't work in a fence line, builders install a stile instead. A stile is a simple set of stairs which allows the walker to go up and over the fence and down on the other side, without touching the fence itself. If sheep ever figure out how to operate a kissing gate or walk up and down the stairs of a stile, the game will be over, but so far, the humans are winning.

At one point we rounded a corner and passed through a kissing gate into a pasture full of sheep. At first, the critters were startled as sheep easily can be, and they ran from us. Slowly, though, their curiosity and the lush grass where we sat brought them back toward us. We sat on nearby stones and watched them for half an hour as they grazed closer and closer to us. "We promised you friendly sheep," we told Claire and Philip.

"What happens to all these wooly guys?" Claire finally asked.

"Are you sure you want to know?" we answer. Claire shrugged. "Shepherd's pie," we said.

"Ohhhh. Did you have to tell me that? I'm not doing too well with the sheep today, am I?"

Around the next large hill and bend in the coast, we walked across a grassy pasture to a deep gorge and ravine. Massive cliffs and fissures gave these headlands a dramatic and powerful feel. The winds increased and came pouring through the gaps as we got farther out along the coast, but the views were spectacular. In fact, these headlands cannot be described or imagined. We were high up above the sea. The rocks and edges of these cliffs were black to the eye, and the waves were crashing onto them below as the tide rose. Salty sea spray blew up around us, enveloping us in a misty cloud. The whole scene made us quiet and reflective, being more sweeping and grand than we expected. The sea pounded away below us, birds hunted for fish cast upon the rocks, and here and there we thought we saw a seal.

Philip and I were strolling along together, lingering behind Mark and Claire who marched ahead of us. "Claire loves this," he told me. "We haven't taken the time to walk along the sea like this for many years." We could see Mark and Claire ahead of us taking turns posing on a huge rock, making statues for each other to photograph. "She hasn't relaxed like this in a long time. I'm glad to see all those instincts come back to her." We could see her doing her best version of the Statue of Liberty with Mark playing the paparazzi for her. Click. Click.

The Coast Path is long and wide, leading out across the treeless hills to the horizon, interrupted only by jutting spikes of granite or here and there a chimney from an old tin mine. After a while, we came to a fork in the path which was well marked by a signpost. One path led away from the sea, back across the moor toward Halsetown. The other pointed toward Zennor. We decided to linger here for a while and try to absorb all that we had seen. With the wind blowing against us, we each found a spot to sit and stare northward, out to the sea. 'I've never seen this before,' I thought to myself, even though I'd been in this very part of the Coast Path half a dozen times in recent years. It all looked new and fresh, as it did each time I visited here.

We were like four monks—or three monks and a nun, to be more precise—as we sat in our solitary meditation, each in our own natural pew. It was like sitting on the edge of the world. What a luxury it was to sit quietly, listening to the rapturous music of the sea, feeling its spray, seeing its power rise and fall on the waves. No monastery chapel can offer quite the same sacred space. I'm not sure how long we all sat with our thoughts that morning, but finally, Claire came over to my spot and sat down next to me, so close that our elbows touched.

"I can't believe we're here," she said quietly as if she were in a church. "I remember that night on our deck last fall when we first made these plans. I just never thought we'd actually make this trip."

She was correct. This whole journey started one evening, innocently enough, with a martini. We were sitting on their deck, munching on appetizer tapas, and sipping our cocktails. It was our old gang back home, and we were a "toasty crowd" so every now and then as we sat there, someone would raise a glass to toast this or that. We toasted the lovely weather that evening, the loons out on the lake, and Philip and Claire for being our hosts. They were celebrating Claire's retirement and Philip's liberation, and they invited their friends in to join them.

"Here's to you, Claire!" Philip had proposed that night. Claire had just finished her final day as a forensic accountant, working in a downtown law firm. Her job was to find people who cheat, and she

19

was good at it. Her specialty was deadbeat spouses trying to end-run the system and avoid post-divorce support payments. It was a busy and hyperactive career, and she'd been moving at a hundred-miles-an-hour for a long time. She had "seen it all," as she put it, and it had made her, may I say, just a little crusty and cynical. The truth is that professionally speaking, she rarely saw a good marriage or an honest guy.

We all raised our glasses to her. She was finally retired, and the two of them were busy figuring out how to live together again. Despite all her bluster, Claire did have a soft spot, and it was Philip. She called him her anchor, not that he slowed or weighed her down, but that he offered stability in her wild, adrenaline-charged world.

For this part, Philip always seemed to take everything with a grain of salt; he was a low-keyed, philosophical type of guy. He offered a calming hand when Claire was in a stormy mood, and their friends could count on him to balance her crazy antics. He had been alone at home for quite a few years while she was out and about with her job—he had become the house husband—but I think he found it lonely and isolating. He told us he felt liberated by having Claire back in the house every day.

Claire, for her part, added much-needed energy to Philip's life. When he slipped into his quiet mode, Philip could quickly fade into the background, but she pulled him out and encouraged him to speak up and get into the conversations. They were a well-matched set.

So that night on their deck when Mark and I toasted our upcoming visit to Cornwall and St Ives, we casually threw out the idea that they should join us. "We've rented a two-bedroom house," we told them. "Why not come?" Before the evening ended, they were on their computer buying tickets.

Claire reminded me as we sat there now on the rocky coast of the Atlantic Ocean that, over that martini, she had pinned her hopes on St Ives. She needed help to get back on a more solid emotional and spiritual footing. She had spent her career dealing with selfish, mean, and dishonest people. She needed a bit of healing, she told me.

"How's it going so far?" I asked her.

"Well, these winds sure blew a lot of crap outta me, that's for sure. You guys are wonderful to show us this place. It's pretty darn magnificent. When I heard you reciting that poetry back there. Who was it? Tennyson, I think you said? I realized that it was about me. For the last few years my ship has been very much out on the sea. Thank goodness for Philip." We chatted on about how she experienced such a high-demand corporate setting. "I was making a lot of money," she told me, "but I was losing my bearings. If it hadn't been for Philip, I'm sure I may have lost my soul altogether. I started to think everything was somehow all about me. But just these first two days here have opened up a whole new vision for me." She put her arm around me, and we just sat there in silence together for a few minutes.

Philip and Mark soon joined us, and we four slowly came back together. As we explored an old stone wall we found on the other side of the hill, we emerged from our solitude and rejoined each other's society. Gradually, however, even in this remarkably beautiful and expansive place, this large outdoor cathedral with its stark and striking beauty, the mundane began to creep in, and we started thinking about lunch.

Chapter 3

The Seafood Café: Speaking of Art

So where to have our lunch? When you're on holiday, this a very important question. There is, of course, an old pub several miles farther west along the Coast Path in Zennor. It's called the Tinners Arms, and it dates all the way back to 1271. There is a cozy log fire there, which would undoubtedly have warmed us after such a windy trek.

Zennor is gorgeous. "At Zennor, one sees infinite Atlantic," D. H. Lawrence wrote in 1916, "all peacock-mingled colors, and the gorse is sunshine itself. Zennor is a most beautiful place: a tiny granite village nestling under high shaggy moor-hills and a big sweep of the lovely sea beyond, such a lovely sea, lovelier even than the Mediterranean...It is the best place I have been in, I think." (Letter of 25 February 1916 to Ottoline Morrell, from *The Collected Letters of D.H. Lawrence*, ed. Harry T. Moore (Heinemann, London: 1962) volume 1, p. 437.) Lawrence spent a couple of years near Zennor during the war. He was there with his wife, Frieda, a German and in fact a cousin to Manfred von Richthofen—the infamous 'Red Barron.' Despite his kind words about the place, their welcome in Zennor wasn't particularly warm; German bombs, after all, were pounding England at the time. Nonetheless, they seem to have been regulars at the Tinners Arms.

This pub, seemingly hidden away in Zennor, five or so miles outside St Ives, can easily be overlooked by visitors. It's warm, cozy, friendly, and filled with a mix of locals, walkers, visitors, well-mannered dogs, and even residents of its four rooms of lodging. When you step into the bar with its massive log fire, you're stepping into an old room where people have held countless conversations amplified by countless pints of ale—for centuries! The menu for the dining room is fantastic: delicious offerings of local lamb and beef, local fish and seafood, and all of it prepared and presented with warm hospitality. It's a pub we shouldn't miss, but five miles by car equals about a four-hour walk along the Coast Path, and our appetites felt more urgent than that.

So, after mounting one very high point, surveying our kingdoms one last time, and counting our sheep, we headed back toward St Ives along the same muddy path we had just followed. On our way back, as often happens, we all saw the headlands and the water as if for the first time. One after the other of us remarked about a point jutting out that we hadn't noticed before or how close the gorse was to the pathway. 'Is this the same path we followed to get here?' We asked rhetorically. It all looked so new. And yet, the walk back to town seemed quicker, and soon we found ourselves within view of St Ives once again. As we rounded the final bend back along the Porthmeor Beach area, we picked up our pace just a little and began to consider some choices for our lunch.

In December, of course, there are fewer visitors to St Ives than in the summer, and fewer of the summer hot spots are open, but that still leaves dozens of excellent choices in wintertime. In recent years the culinary scene here has been energetic and active. There's an abundance of seafood, local lamb, and poultry. I once counted more than seventy-five options for dining, ranging from romantic to casual. We had our pick for lunch. There were delis, fish & chip shops galore, ice cream parlors (OK, maybe after lunch), burger bars, tea rooms, pasty shops, vegetarian cafés, and Asian takeaways. There were several pubs in town with all-day food menus, and there were also a handful of excellent gastropubs in the surrounding countryside such as the Tinners Arms, or farther down the road, The Gurnard's Head. The choice was ours!

We surveyed each other in our group of four and decided we were all hoping for a short nap afterward so the lunch could be simple— maybe even a bowl of soup. We turned off the flats onto the Digey and walked toward the center of town.

The Digey is some 20 yards long, running from Fore Street to Back Road through the center of the village. On the lower end, nearest the beach, is the Alfred Wallis Cottage, a beautiful stone building in which Wallis himself retired, and after the death of his wife he painted there for twenty years. He lived in poverty his entire life, painting on cardboard torn from packing boxes—he couldn't afford canvases—and with a minimal palette of oils. Eventually, other famous St Ives artists—including Nicholson and Hepworth among others—discovered his work and helped him get noticed. You can see his paintings in the Tate now. He mainly became famous posthumously.

Across the Digey from the Wallis house is Bumbles Tea Room, a bright and cheery spot for breakfast and a landmark on that corner. Across from Bumbles is a tiny residential cottage which we have rented in the past. It's as cute as a bug's nest, but the ceiling height is just a bit lower than my six-foot, two-inch frame. I spent the entire week ducking. A few steps farther down the Digey are Number 21 with a bright blue door and Number 24 with a very old-looking Dutch door. Other doorways along the Digey hide bed and breakfasts, private lodgings, and self-catering cottages. Our doorway was next. Our cottage was known locally as the "Corner Cottage," but we aren't sure how it got that name since this house is nowhere near any corner; in fact, it's in the middle of the block. We refer to it only as our "fisherman's cottage."

A bit farther down the Digey is Rose Lane off to the left, a narrow lane filled with windows covered with lace curtains and doorways marked by pots of flowers. Just beyond Rose Lane is the Digey Food Room where local folks, as well as tourists, show up every day for soups and lunches. Maybe that would be our stop today. Hot soup, close to home, a comfy café—what else could we want?

A step or two beyond the Food Room is Fore Street, but we turned to the right before we got that far and followed Virgin Lane around

26

the corner and up the steep hill where the city has located that cemetery which we saw from the Coast Path. Doorways and tiny passageways crowd Virgin Lane leading to even more doorways beyond. It's picturesque and charming. The entire lane has cobblestone pavement and granite gutters, and we imagined that in the rain, this might be a small river. Residents have carefully planted the lane with heather, geraniums, and small pines. Along the way, we eventually passed through a very narrow space, just as wide as one person, and up a steep granite stair which landed us on Barnawoon Street. We were up at the top of this part of town now, but the climb wasn't quite over. Finally, huffing and puffing just a little, we came to Clodgy View, the lane which runs along a large car park and ends at the city cemetery. We were up above and looking down on the enormous Tate now, high above the sea. There wasn't a restaurant in sight up here.

"So, lunch," Philip began. "Are we near our lunch?"

"Well actually, no. We thought you'd like to see this place first. It gives you such a great view of the Coast Path. Isn't it gorgeous? Sometimes you just have to go where the beauty is, Philip. Lunch, munch. We'll find a spot on the way down the hill."

"I see a bench," Claire said. "I'm sitting down." Indeed, there was a single bench up there, on the grassy knoll inside the cemetery's granite wall, just big enough for four if we squeezed a little.

"If we have time later, we can wander through this cemetery," we told them. "Alfred Wallis is buried up here, among other local famous types." An elaborate gravestone, depicting a tiny mariner at the foot of a lighthouse—a popular motif in Wallis' paintings—

was made from tiles by the potter Bernard Leach. It covers Wallis' tomb. Whole families of fishers and sailors have plots up here. They spent their lives on the sea, and now they're gazing out at it for eternity. Cool. We gradually let go of lunch long enough to spend half an hour on that bench, resting and gabbing and chatting.

And then the rain began. It started out as only a light mist; then the skies turned from azure to grey. When the sky became suddenly even darker, we realized we'd better get moving down the hill. Sure enough, before we got back to that steep, granite stairway, it was a light rain. Did we ever remember to carry our umbrellas? Down Barnawoon we scampered—it turns out running downhill is much easier than uphill—and soon we were back at Fore Street. We turned right and hugged the buildings to keep dry as we went. Fore Street is yet another cobbled lane, full of small shops selling nougat or pasties or trinkets for tourists. People were bustling along, Christmas on their minds, while above us along the street, dozens of blue-lighted three-foot evergreen trees had been mounted on the sides of each building, pointing out at an angle. Above the street itself was a canopy of lights that followed the curves of the old road, twinkling and blinking in the cloudy and rainy midday. Very cheery, we agreed, rain notwithstanding, and our steps were a little lighter now that we were out of the mud and off the hill.

About five minutes down Fore Street brought us to the door of the Seafood Café, a modern-looking restaurant a couple of steps below street level. It was warm and inviting, and we very quickly decided to eat there. "They might have a seafood chowder," Mark said, still planning on a mere bowl of soup.

We hustled in out of the rain, which was now driven by the wind and lashing against the door of the Café. As we brushed off our wet coats and settled down to our table, Claire noticed the specials board and announced that the soup, in her case, would have to wait; she was ordering the seared local scallops appetizer, just to get started. The menu said that the chef would serve these with crisp chorizo and an artichoke puree. That sounded pretty good to all of us. I hated to see her eat alone, so I ordered my first course of chargrilled sardines on pesto toast. I'm a sucker for a good sardine. Philip ordered the mussels starter. These would be local, Cornish mussels, and the chef here prepared them in white wine, garlic, shallots, and coriander. Mark was in luck; the soup of the day was indeed chowder, but he ordered only an appetizer portion.

So much for a simple lunch and a nap. We all settled in as we awaited our first courses but not before we ordered a bottle of the Re Paolo Fiano from Italy. It was a delicious Sicilian white wine, bright, aromatic, and crisp. It was served just a little too chilled, so our first taste didn't reveal all the citrus it had in it, but as it warmed to cellar temp on our table, the wine finished perfectly. A toast to the Coast Path came first, then one to the hill we had just climbed.

"To the rain," Claire chimed in. "You gotta have a little rain, or you aren't really living an honest life."

"You hate the rain," Philip turned to her.

"I know, but I liked *this* rain. I hated the rain when I was in a business suit and trying to get somewhere fast. I hated snow just as much. But now," Claire changed her tone, "the rain makes me feel romantic." It was splashing against the windows of the Café, but inside, it was light and cozy and warm. Philip leaned in and gave her a little kiss.

"To each other."

"Here's a toast to this first great hike of the week. We were tired, but it had been a lovely morning together."

The wine was delicious, but wait! What were we thinking? We had planned to make this a quick lunch, followed by a long nap. What happened? Well, we had bustled ourselves into a warm and cozy café, coming in out of the rain, and found ourselves among other diners, amid the buzz and chatter of the room, with a display cabinet full of fresh fish and poultry. It just seemed wrong somehow to order only a bowl of soup and, afterward, to trudge back out into the rain. Plus, Claire started it! It was all her fault. She abandoned our plan first, and the rest of us were merely sweet to go along with her lead. So, we sipped on our wine while we awaited our first course. Mark and I knew that this meal would be excellent; it wasn't our first visit to this café.

"I can't get over all the art in this town," Philip said. "I heard you mention Alfred Wallis, but I don't know who that is, to be honest." Mark and I didn't know much more than Philip about Wallis even though we'd been visiting here for many years. How did all this get started here? Philip wanted to know. "Why here?" He asked. "And why the Tate? Why would the Tate come to a little fishing village at the end of the road? As we were driving down from London the other day, it felt like we were leaving the urban behind, but this place has a very urban vibe. Don't you agree, Claire?"

"I think the vibe here is urban-exile," Claire said. "From what I can see, a lot of these people and most of these artists were escaping urban life and styles to create their own world out here. Didn't you say that Barbara Hepworth lived here? I'm pretty sure she was looking for a place where she could do whatever the hell she wanted. I mean, for a woman at the time, she'd had a couple of marriages, right? And some kids? And she was working in a man's world, but out here it was her world. She made it her world.

"So now the town has filled up with artists, right? Galleries all over town?"

"And a lot of artist wannabes, to be honest."

"Ugh. Artists," Mark said.

"But you're one, Honey."

"Well, I'm sure I could be shot for saying this, but not everything in all these shops is art. A lot of it is tourist seascape stuff. The painter had one idea, and she kept repeating it over and over again." Claire winced. "Or *he*," he added. "But a lot of it has a feminine feel, which isn't bad in and of itself, but I think it's created to sell to women who go around these seaside towns carrying designer bags and buying art," he said using air quotes.

"The thing is, there is some exquisite art here, and there has been for a long time. Maybe I'm a purist about this, but it seems to me that mass-producing works for a popular market isn't really art. It's decorating. Most artists aren't that self-conscious. They simply paint, or sculpt, or make pottery. They're not doing art to sell as much as they're trying to follow their muse."

Like who? Who's still around town these days?"

"Well, believe it or not, you can still buy original art here from the old school. Hepworth comes up for sale quite often, not her enormous works but smaller ones, including sketches. Wallis is for sale sometimes. But also others. I've seen Barrie Cook and Terry Frost for sale. And there's this woman, Wilhelmina—I think her last name is something like Barn or something like that."

"Barns-Graham, I think it is. Isn't that right?"

"Maybe. She's dead of course, but you still see her gouaches come up for sale now and then. This is real art, substantial art. And there's this fellow, Keith Varney, I think it is, who is actually not from St Ives. He's from Bath, but he was mentored by Corina Ciscato, and they're part of a sculptural porcelain school. His work is architectural and quite beautiful. He hand-builds each piece. Or the Raku guy. Is it Peter Hayes? Something like that? His work is pricey, but wow, it's gorgeous art. And there are others, lots of others…"

"Ah," Philip the philosopher jumped in. "The age-old argument: *What is art?* I saw what you wrote on your website, Mark. You said that for you, painting is an expression of your inner heart and mind. You called it a language, how you talk about what you see around you, a way of expressing your thoughts and feelings. I think it's very intimate for you, isn't it?"

"Well, it is. I do realize that money is part of this. You gotta pay the rent. But when I see someone mass-producing one art concept just because it sells fast, that doesn't seem like art to me, even if it keeps them in business. I'll be interested in what you see when you get into the shops around town."

And at this point, the waiter arrived to get our order for the main course. If we'd been having a full-fledged evening meal, we would have trekked over to their display case and chosen our fish or poultry from their current selections. Then we would have selected a sauce for it, based on what the chef was offering that night, all scribbled daily onto a blackboard. But since this was "just lunch" we postponed that for another visit and ordered off the menu. Mark and I decided to share an order of the crab linguini; this would be hand-picked Cornish crab in garlic and lemon butter. Yum. Claire ordered the warm chicken and bacon salad while Philip chose the seafood pie. His mussels first course would be pretty light, and this pie would be full of white fish, haddock, and prawns, topped with parmesan mash. How could he go wrong? "Oh yes, and a second bottle of wine, if you please," we told the waiter.

"Oh, good grief," someone said. "We really are going to need those naps, aren't we?"

"Well, we walked to the end of the earth and climbed to the top of the mountain today," Claire said. "We need to have our electrolytes replenished." She was very matter of fact.

"Oh, for Pete's sake, Claire," Mark told her. "You do that by drinking water, not wine. But what the hell, the wine's here; we might as well drink it." We were easy to please.

Over the meal, we returned to our conversation about art. As the relativist in the bunch, Claire argued—between bites of her salad—that art's value belongs to each person. What's art to one person might be trash to another. Beauty is subjective, not objective, she told us. You can't argue taste, as the saying goes. But in fact, I argued, there are some standards of judgment about art, not so strict as to edge out exciting or new forms of expression, but enough to be able to say that, in the eye of most people, rubbish is rubbish. Beauty might be considered a consensus idea, I felt. When the consensus is that a painting is valuable, then it is. Its price goes up as that consensus spreads.

So, if some rich tourist with an expensive handbag came through town and bought a mass-produced watercolor of a sailboat on the harbor because she thought the blue in it would match the colors of her bathroom at home, well, that would be her choice. And I guess that to her, it would also be artsy enough to please her.

We went back and forth on this argument, but we were starting to grow weary, and we didn't appear to be moving toward a resolution on any of this. We agreed it might be best if we all had that nap now. So, after we'd eaten this meal and had our electrolytes fully restored, we were all ready to finally head back to the cottage, a short five-minute walk. In fact, I think our sleepy brains were one of the reasons all our arguments on art ran afoul.

We paid our bill and stepped outside to find that the rain had ended, leaving freshly washed streets and dappled light behind. But as we left the restaurant and returned to Fore Street, we accidentally turned left instead of right and walked down to Ayr

Lane before we realized it. We may have been in a bit of a wine-induced daze. We were about to turn around when Claire noticed a sign pointing to the Barbara Hepworth museum, just a few steps up Ayr Lane. "Let's just go and see what this is about," she said and promptly marched up Ayr Lane with the three of us following obediently.

"You can kiss your nap goodbye," Philip whispered as we walked up Ayr and turned right toward the museum. Before we knew it, just a few steps up the hill, we found ourselves at the gate of the Barbara Hepworth Museum and Gardens.

Chapter 4
Dame Barbara Hepworth

Barbara Hepworth is one of the UK's most celebrated sculptors. She and her four children made St Ives their home; Hepworth lived here from 1939 until her death in 1975. These were her peak years, and she achieved quite great fame during this time. She represented Britain at the Venice Biennale, for example, and she designed the gigantic sculpture in the United Nations Plaza in New York. It's called simply, *Single Form (BH 325)*, and it's a monumental bronze sculpture; easily her most significant work. It has been on display in New York since 1964 as a memorial to Dag Hammarskjöld, the UN Secretary-General who died after an air crash in Africa in 1961.

She lived in St Ives, but Barbara Hepworth was famous. Her presence helped turn this remote town and former fishing village located nearly at the end of England into that thriving artists' community which we discussed at lunch. Other artists or artist-wannabes moved here to be part of the movement that circulated around Hepworth and her cronies.

We had walked up the short hill to the museum past the back gate of the Union Inn, past dumpsters and workers' entrances, and past delivery docks for shops and restaurants. It wasn't so much an alley as a side street. The entrance to the Hepworth Museum was rather plain: a simple wooden door in a stone wall with a modest sign beside it. It belied the significance of the artist whose work it housed.

But we had a decision to make. We'd just had a long morning of muddy hiking along the Atlantic coast, faced down a flock of timid sheep, and enjoyed a long and languorous lunch with two bottles of wine and a lot of seafood. Now we were presented with Dame Hepworth and her beautiful collection of sculpture. Do we nap, or do we not? Before we could answer, Claire had paid for the tickets, wandered into the museum, and started reading the story of Hepworth's life. Knowing Claire, there was no turning back now, so we all dived in together, wandering through her house, her gardens, her sculptures, her life story, and her mind. We even wandered among her tools which were laying on the tables, just where she had left them. The place had the look of a studio that she had only left briefly to go find some coffee.

She was a remarkable woman and artist. Her work may well be the single most outstanding example of Modernism and in particular, modern sculpture. Very few female artists in those years hoped to achieve international prominence, but she stood tall among them. Claire was keen to learn about her.

The downstairs museum told her life story while her upstairs studio was filled with abstract works. Her works reflect her character, we think. They curl and twist gently and are often pierced by a hole. They have kind angles and bends. Her style is unmistakable and reminded us of one of her quotes which we had read, "I, the sculptor, am the landscape." Outside was her garden in which she often entertained local artists, always as Dame Barbara, always a gracious 'lady of the house.' Children played among her works. There was once a sign in her studio that read: "Please do touch."

She had studied at the Royal College of Art, which is the only entirely postgraduate art and design university in the world, under a scholarship rarely offered to a woman. After she graduated in 1925, she journeyed to Florence. As Claire read this note aloud, she fully understood the challenges Hepworth faced as a female in an otherwise mostly male trade. Florence, of course, had been home to Michelangelo and many other sculptors, but all males. Why not Hepworth now? It seemed so fitting that she would have gotten her impulse to sculpt there in Florence, the epicenter of 15th and 16th-century marble.

She married John Skeaping there in 1925, and they lived for a short time in Italy. Skeaping had been born in South Woodford, Essex. He studied at both Goldsmith's College in London and the Royal Academy. He was in Italy while Barbara was there because he had won the British *Prix de Rome* in 1924 and the prize included a scholarship to the British School at Rome.

In Italy, Hepworth studied carving under the master sculptor, Giovanni Ardini. She and Skeaping returned to London in 1926 where they continued to work both alone and together, turning their flat into a sort of salon and studio. They had a son together named Paul, who was born in London in 1929. Tragically, he was killed in 1953 in a plane crash while serving with the Royal Air Force in Thailand. She carved a memorial to him which now stands in the Lady Chapel of the parish church here in St. Ives. It's called *Madonna and Child* and is an intimate image of a child being held close by his mother, their arms around each other in a permanent embrace of love.

How interesting that her most important work was a sculpture to honor a man who died in an airplane crash—Dag Hammarskjold— and her most intimate sculpture was to honor another man who died in the same way, this one her son.

After their divorce, Skeaping worked for a while in Mexico and eventually retired in Devon and the Camargue. Eight of his works are in the Tate in St Ives.

Hepworth was involved both in England and on the continent in every significant modern art movement of the age. She met and knew Jean Arp, Pablo Picasso, and Constantin Brâncuşi, a Romanian sculptor living in France who was known as the patriarch of modern sculpture. At the time she met them, she was traveling with Ben Nicholson, who would come to play a significant role in her life. Her work to promote modernism and

British art, in particular, cannot be overstated. She was an active force and worked with nearly every leading figure of that movement.

After divorcing Skeaping, she lived for a time with Ben Nicholson—with whom she had triplets—and they married in 1938. She divorced him in 1951, but they had moved here to St Ives long before that. Her studio was called Trewyn. The climate of the place and the space in this studio were her dream workspace. And St Ives was for her, as for many others, a refuge from World War II. The didactic in the museum quotes her saying, "Finding Trewyn Studio was sort of magic. Here was a studio, a yard, and a garden where I could work in open air and space."

"I'm starting to understand this," Philip told us. "These artists landed here by hook or by crook, found each other, loved the light and the sea, and that's why this happened. It *evolved*." He said.

"It's what I was saying in the Café," Claire added. "This isn't London or New York, and that's the point. In a place like this where everyone's a little bit of a misfit, anyone can advance— women, homosexuals, immigrants—they had 'em all here."

"*Homosexuals*?" Mark asked. "Really?"

"Well, that's the word they used. I'm trying to be historical."

Claire had been narrating this museum visit. She read most of the didactic aloud, adding her own editorial material to it. We were all learning a lot about Ms. Hepworth and her friends, but I was beginning at this point to get a bit dull-headed with weariness and the effects of the wine. "I have to pee," I finally said, and traipsed off to find a bathroom. Afterward, I wandered into a central area where I found a comfortable chair with my name on it. As I sat down, Claire and her entourage—Mark, Philip, and two or three other visitors who liked her narration—came around the corner, and the story continued.

We learned that Hepworth (with Nicholson) had been a co-founder of the Penwith Society of Arts along with nineteen other artists. Among them was Peter Lanyon who was born here in St Ives. He was a talented landscape painter, helping launch a critical reappraisal of modernism. He died at age 46 and is buried out at Lelant, along the road to St Just. Another co-founder of the Penwith Society was Bernard Leach, who went on to become St Ives' most famous potter. His studio is now open to the public. Penwith was a breakaway group, leaving the more conservative St Ives School. Both schools survived and are active today in St Ives.

There's a photo of Ms. Hepworth there in the 1960s, her later years. By this time, she looked like a Cornish miner, dark and rough—and many of those miners were, in fact, women! She held a cigarette in one hand and her chisel in the other. She looked small compared to the sculpture on which she was working, small but powerful. She used this garden for many of her large projects, and they still stand here today. The garden is filled with flowers, and most of the bronzes are in the positions in which she placed them. She wanted this garden to become a permanent museum after her death, and so it has. She designed this space with help from a friend, the composer Priaulx Rainier.

We felt as though we were meeting her in her works. Claire stumbled on a quote from one of Ms. Hepworth's diaries: "I rarely draw what I see. I draw what I feel in my body." That became obvious as we wandered among her works. Being in her space— her intimate and personal space—and being unhurried, was completely relaxing. We felt we were, in a sense, in her hands, just as her hammer and chisel had been.

But, as exciting and beautiful as this place was, we had finally reached the end of our collective ropes, and we agreed to head home. We said on our way back down the hill as we turned left onto Fore Street to head back to our cottage that we could not believe we had nearly missed this museum. "I told you guys," Claire said. "I said it would be good. You gotta learn to trust ole' Claire." We all agreed. In fact, it was almost better than lunch, we said—but nothing could stop us now from getting our naps.

Chapter 5
The Journey

We four intrepid travelers had arrived—punchy and groggy from the long flight— in St Ives just one day before this hike and lunch. As I mentioned, we were here to celebrate the Christmas holidays. In part, we hoped to escape the crazy consumerism and constant advertising about Christmas that goes on in America. We were all fed up with that guy on TV intoning, "Just thirteen more shopping days until Christmas." Mark and I were eager to introduce our friends to Cornwall and St Ives. Philip and Claire seemed the perfect companions. They love England: Philip loves the hedgerows and the countryside, the small villages, the gastropubs, and the parish churches; Claire loves the history here, the commitment to slow change, and the Queen: she's a dyed-in-the-wool monarchist. They both liked the idea of being here for Christmas.

In any case, we had landed at Heathrow about noon London time two days ago. We decided to work our way through immigration and customs as quickly as we could, pick up our rental car, and drive west on the M4—just to get out of town. Mark and I knew a pub within half an hour of the airport, so we headed in that direction. Traffic was light as we passed Slough, Maidenhead, and Reading and at Theale in the Berkshires, we took the exit onto Bath Road from which we quickly shifted over onto High Street where we pulled into the car park for the Bull Pub.

We hadn't slept much on the plane; we were tired and a bit bleary-eyed. But when we slipped into the Bull and had a seat in the friendly dining room, with the smell of lunch in the air and other diners noisily preceding us, all that fatigue faded and we replaced it with the excitement and comfort of our first pub lunch of the trip. And it was a dandy. We started with a shared plate to calm our airplane-induced hunger: a warm chèvre served with delicious homemade onion chutney and crusty bread. We had spotted a herd of goats just as we left the M4 and we wondered if this cheese may have come from them. We devoured the cheese and bread as though we hadn't eaten in many days! Four pints of ale helped wash it down. And of course, a series of toasts preceded the meal.

"Here's to being on the ground," Philip began. "It's great to be here."

"And here's to those plucky goats. This chèvre is magnificent."

"And to that woman at the car rental who gave us the upgrade. Bless her little heart."

The rest of the lunch was just as delicious as our opener: fish and chips, sausage and mash, steak and kidney pie, and an unbelievably good pork belly mulled in cider and served with dauphinoise potatoes. Ah yes, we said as we wiped our mouths for the last time, we've landed now. And while we were all victims of a little jet lag, we swore a pact to stay awake until we arrived at our bed and breakfast, two hours farther down the road. Even then, we agreed, we'd wait until English bedtime so that we'd awaken on English daytime in the morning.

For us Americans, or maybe I should say, Americans from the Upper Midwest, there is something endlessly inviting and enticing about an authentic English pub like the Bull. Mark and I keep a list of them handy, so we can pull one out almost anywhere in the UK. We're drawn to them because we know when we enter it will be as it is today: the room will be warm and the people friendly. We do have warm places and friendly people galore in the Upper Midwest. In fact, "Minnesota nice" is our brand name up there. But in England, the pubs are more than merely friendly places. They play a significant role in the community, and people almost consider the hearth in their neighborhood pub to be part of their home. It's where they have a sense of belonging.

Historically, pubs were local public houses; hence the name. They served as public living rooms where everyone could gather, including the children and dogs. They have always been a place geared towards social interaction. The drinking, while not incidental, is optional and isn't the main point. The purpose of the pub is to provide a place for people to meet each other.

Maybe the age of the pubs is what gets us. Very few buildings in our home state are older than 1850, but most are newer than 1920—we tend to tear down old buildings. But remember the pub in Zennor just outside St Ives, the Tinners Arms? It's been in business continually since 1217, and that's true for many pubs across England. Maybe this age-old presence in the community has endowed them with unique spiritual powers to lure us in and, once there, to comfort us.

At any rate, after that first lunch, we jumped back on the M4 and journeyed onward past Bristol and onto the M5 southward toward Exeter. We stopped at a bed and breakfast that we had arranged in Weston-super-Mare for the night. All of us needed a good night's sleep. The following day we knew that our little fisherman's cottage in St Ives would be available at about 2 PM.

Indeed, it was ready and waiting. The women who manage this cottage had come in before us and trimmed it up for Christmas. They had hung stars in the windows, tucked Christmas lights and tchotchkes into every shelf and window sill—an elf here and a reindeer there—and a bottle of champagne was standing on the table with a welcome note. Christmas was in the air! We hauled in our luggage, some groceries we had bought on the way, and two jumbo packs of Christmas crackers. A little cheer went up among us to finally be there, the long plane ride and 300-mile car trip now behind us. Our journey had delivered us to this cozy fisherman's cottage, and we were finally at home in St Ives.

Philip's first self-assigned task was to examine the kitchen in detail. Like a chef—and Philip had worked as a professional chef for many years before he became their homemaker—he opened every cupboard and door in the room, exclaiming here and there that, yes, this will do nicely, or sometimes not. He and Mark unpacked the groceries like store clerks, including the spices and herbs they had carried with them. They had managed to fill up the refrigerator and cupboards with provisions for the week ahead.

"You aren't arranging everything in the kitchen alphabetically, are you?" I asked. At home, our spice shelf was in perfect alphabetical order at all times. Before I knew Mark, I used a somewhat more casual system for spices: I merely shoved everything into the cupboard. What I used often floated to the front; what I never used got pushed to the back. Once a year or so, I went through everything in the back row and discarded what had gotten out of date. Simple.

The truth is that Mark's system in our kitchen worked very well. He was the lead cook in our family while I took care of the ambiance. I suppose you could say that one's home is a picture of the inside of one's head, and we like ours with low lights, romantic music, and a spot near every seat to set down a glass of wine or sparkling water. We loved sharing meals with friends and almost always chose that over going out. Mark tended the kitchen, and I took care of the hospitality. It had been working like a charm for us for more than twenty years.

Meanwhile, back at the cottage, Claire had disappeared briefly and was moving in by unpacking every single item she and Philip had brought with them, putting them all away in their drawers and closet, and hiding their suitcases under their bed. "Now I'm here," she announced when she came downstairs. 'OK then,' I thought. 'I'd better hustle if I want to catch up to her.' I unpacked for the week just like I managed the spices: I piled up some things in one spot in the room and other stuff in another. I used one entire side of the room to organize myself for the week. Piles were my strategy: a collection of socks here, boxers there, and my Christmas things were all in a single place. It worked for me.

By the time I came back downstairs to the living room, Philip had opened a map of St Ives and was trying to figure out where we were on it. None of the streets or lanes in this village come out where one thinks they might, however. They wind and dodge their way through the town, sometimes heading up this hill or around that old public monument. St Ives and its streets were here long before autos and trucks, and everyone who lives here knows how to find their way around.

Meanwhile, Claire had unfolded one of those large Michelin maps of England. It was map #503 covering Wales, the Midlands, and Southwest England. It was a large map, at least four feet in each direction, and it included everything from Liverpool and Manchester in the North to Penzance here in the Southwest. It was hopelessly vague and, even if folded down to show only Cornwall, it still had tiny print and only the main roads.

"I don't think those maps are going to help you much," I said. "The only way to discover this place is to explore it and make a lot of mistakes. Let's go. I'm eager to get moving."

"Oh, just hang on a minute. Don't be so map negative," she said. "Just because you've been here before doesn't mean you know *everything*. Maybe I'll find something new, even to you."

"I've just been scolded," I said. "I think it might be the jetlag."

"Oh, you," she said. "I'm taking my map to the kitchen." And she left the room. 'Well,' I thought to myself, 'that didn't go very well. I'd better keep my mouth shut.'

"Welcome to the family, Bill," Philip said.

I think we came to St Ives, not so much to be away from our home in Minnesota, as to make sharing with these friends even more intimate. We're not just sharing a single evening and supper with Claire and Philip, but a whole week of a shared bathroom and kitchen and all the stuff of daily life. As we started out, we were all hoping for the best. Maybe I didn't get us off to a perfect start. I followed her to the kitchen.

"Can I make you a cup of tea?" I asked.

"Is this make-up tea?"

"It is."

"OK, then I want Earl Grey with a little honey and one of those ginger cookies we bought if you please. And use one of those pretty cups hanging there," she said, pointing to the cupboard. Philip and Mark soon joined us, and before long, we were all looking at the maps, making plans, and sipping tea together.

"So why St Ives? How did you ever find this place down here at the very end of England?" Philip asked. It was a good question because we'd been hanging around this old fishing village for nearly two decades, but we'd never really thought about why we'd chosen this particular place. The world is full of small villages.

The places we visit shape our lives. We journey to other towns or nations because we want to be touched by them and to let them change how we view the reality of our lives at home. To some extent, travel opens us up to the people of other cultures. "It is necessary, especially for Americans, to see other lands and experience other cultures," Maya Angelou wrote in 1993. "The American, living in this vast country and able to traverse three thousand miles east to west using the same language, needs to hear languages as they collide in Europe, Africa, and Asia." This is also true for the English, the French, Guatemalans, Cambodians, and people of every culture. If we can't travel in person, we can go there in our armchairs by reading travel stories or watching them on other media.

A visitor here in St Ives who is browsing through a clothing store, for example, might very well hear people speaking in one of a dozen different languages. Visitors come here from around the world. Hearing others speak their own languages helps us remember that the world is vast and we're only a small part of it. Or it might help us see the world as that proverbial global village in which we must all get along together. Other people—no matter the color of their skin or the language they speak—are quite similar to us. "Perhaps travel cannot prevent bigotry," Angelou said in that same book (*Wouldn't Take Nothing for My Journey*), "but by demonstrating that all peoples cry, laugh, eat, worry, and die, it can introduce the idea that if we try to understand each other, we may even become friends."

The late Anthony Bourdain seemed to agree with Ms. Angelou. "If I'm an advocate for anything," he once wrote, "it's to move. As far as you can, as much as you can. Across the ocean, or simply across the river. The extent to which you can walk in someone else's shoes or at least eat their food is a plus for everybody. Open your mind, get up off the couch, move."

But why St Ives? We had come to realize over the years that, in a way, St Ives found us. Our dear friend, Joan, had mentioned the place to us many years ago, knowing how much we love England. We decided to take her advice and make an initial trip. We immediately felt utterly at home. We weren't sure why the whole experience of visiting England, traveling through the countryside, eating and drinking in the pubs, and feeling so at home there pleased us so much. It was a mystery to us. Furthermore, while England calls us in this way, so do other places.

On one of our first visits to Antigua, Guatemala, Mark and I made a purchase offer on a four-bedroom, three-fountain house. We had fallen in love with the soft earth-toned colors of the city, with fountains, courtyards, and *El Mercado de Antigua*. "Why not stay?" we asked. We thought we'd learn Spanish, figure out how to live through earthquakes, and become expats. Fortunately, the German Fraulein who owned the house refused to negotiate on the price, and we walked away from it. 'Oh, my goodness,' we later said to each other, 'we almost bought a house in Guatemala! *What were we thinking?*'

We love our home in Minnesota, but we're always imagining ourselves living somewhere else. Does everyone do this? One time we were staying for two weeks in Somerset, or maybe it was Dorset, and we found ourselves stopping at the window displays of real estate agents and giving serious thought to living there forever. Only two days of torrential rains knocked some sense into our heads and prevented us from going further at that time.

At any rate, without having to purchase any property, here we were at home now in St Ives for Christmas. Claire had unpacked and moved in. Philip and Mark had commandeered the kitchen. I had found the placemats and linen napkins, the candle holders, and the music system. And, most importantly, we had had and survived our first little quarrel. At home, indeed.

Chapter 6
St Mawgan and the Nuns

On our journey between last night's bed and breakfast and this cottage today we managed to stop for lunch in the village of St Mawgan, just off the A39 near Newquay here in Cornwall. Mark and I know this village. We stumbled into it several years ago on Boxing Day and wound up joining the entire town rugby team in the Falcon Pub for drinks that day. We still aren't entirely sure how that happened, but it was a lot of fun. The publican felt sorry enough for us that he offered us hot pasties for lunch, even though he had closed the kitchen; it was Boxing Day after all. We washed them down, of course, with a pint of local ale. We paused first to toast the roaring fire, the kind publican, and the rugby team. But then we downed the pasties as though they were the last bits of food on earth.

A pasty is essentially a turnover about the size of your hand filled with meat, potatoes, swede, and a little bit of gravy. You eat them hot but with your hands. They were an invention of clever housewives during the mining period in Cornwall's history. The tin miners carried hot pasties wrapped in newspaper down into the mines with them, tucked inside their coats. They kept the miners warm during the chilly mornings, and they were ready at lunchtime: a full meal. In the Falcon that day, it made a perfect lunch for the rugby team and us.

Rugby's a popular sport here in Cornwall. On the day we were in town, it was the St Mawgan team versus the St Austell Sinners. The goal of rugby like any similar sport is to score, but the rules can be challenging to understand for the casual observer. For instance, during the game, while the players move forward toward their goal, the ball cannot be passed forward. The only direction a player can pass is *backward* to his teammates while he moves forward. OK, then. And the player carrying the ball can frequently be tackled. However, once tackled, he is required to release the ball by passing it or moving away from it. Uh-huh. Right. It's a very muddy and physical and adrenaline-producing game and the players who followed us into the Falcon Pub that day were dirty, loud, and ready for beer. Did I mention muddy?

The beer and pasties helped to calm them all down, and being calm is not something for which rugby players are usually known. We hung in there, looking in our tweedy jackets and scarves like preppy college professors doing some sort of sociological study.

Luckily, we didn't get beat up before the adrenaline wore off. We had a blast.

Before we left town that year, we wandered across the road from the pub into what looked like the grounds of a school of some kind. In fact, it was a real, live Carmelite monastery with a community of nuns living in it. The monastery flock of chickens was pecking about on the grounds, and we could see gardens and orchards beyond the walls. Carmelites are a 12th-century religious order in which the members spend a lot of time in contemplation. What sets them apart, though, is that for them, reflection leads them to the people beyond their walls.

The door to a public area of their monastery was open, so we stepped inside. There was a permanent sign hanging there, and it explained who they are: "What we call "Carmel" is a way of life in which we try to be aware of the presence of God in the most ordinary, everyday things. (Even rugby? I wondered.) We're contemplative, but we serve the world. We're prayerful, but we're also practical. We were founded 800 years ago on a mountaintop, but we have our feet firmly planted in today's concerns." 'Hmmm,' I thought, 'that's refreshingly modern.'

We stepped into their public chapel that day and found a remarkably sacred and quiet space where some of the cloistered sisters were keeping a vigil in candlelight and incense from behind their screened enclosure. We couldn't see them, but we knew they were there. The contemplative life is often misunderstood as a withdrawal from the world and its distractions. In fact, though, these women were very "distracted" by the world, in a good way. They were following the needs of the people around them in prayer, something which has gone out of style these days. In their sublime and silent chapel, one could not help but focus and center oneself on beauty, love, and peace. Rather than removing us from the cares of the world around us that day, it re-oriented us toward good. It reminded us that light is stronger than darkness, hope is more forceful than despair, and love is more powerful than all the hate in the world. Silent and quiet, yes, but out of touch, no.

Nonetheless, it was a notable contrast to the rowdy rugby players across the street! Maybe the nuns had prayed for victory against the Sinners because St Mawgan had won the match.

St Mawgan is in a vale, the Vale of Mawgan, which is a beautiful valley through which runs the River Menalhyl. A large field of daffodils was blooming at the top of the vale that day and down below, just across the river from the pub and monastery, is a Japanese Garden, of all things. We are drawn to this village, not only for its pub but also for its general unspoiled beauty. So, as we sailed down the A30 with Claire and Philip on this trip, driving from Exeter to St Ives, we pulled off to share a Christmassy pub lunch in front of a log fire and to revisit the nuns. We weren't disappointed.

We pulled into the car park behind the pub and, before long, the staff at the Falcon was serving us a delicious, homemade lunch consisting of their specialty sandwiches on granary bread. Claire ordered the sausage and caramelized red onion, which she shared with Philip who chose the bacon, brie, and cranberry. Mark and I split two between us as well, the Cornish crab with lemon and dill mayonnaise which was truly sensational, and their excellent hand-carved honey roast ham with English mustard. We had no business doing this, but we weren't in a huge hurry at this point, so why not wash down our lunch with a drop of ale from the local Dartmoor or St Austell breweries? We each ordered a pint. This little ivy-covered pub was busy for lunch the day we were there. The Falcon is a traditional village inn with a roaring fire, wooden beams, and an award-winning garden. Everyone and every dog is welcome. There are two small guest rooms in the Inn, and we've always thought one day we might lodge there.

After placing our order and retrieving our pints from the bar, we huddled around a table just a few feet from the log fire. Two dogs lay on the hearth looking like they'd just come in from central casting. The pub had been decorated for the holidays with Christmas lights that twinkled each time the door opened, and the wind swept in briefly. Other diners had gathered at nearby tables, and the whole place was festive. The light misty rain outside the windows only made the pub cozier and warmer.

There was a momentary silence as we each took a long draw from our pint. "I've got a question," Philip leaned forward. "Why do you think we're here?"

"You mean here in this pub drinking ale?" He shook his head. "You mean why are we here on this planet, as in the big, existential bit about the meaning of life?"

"No, no. I mean why are we here in Cornwall on this holiday? Why are we traveling away from our perfectly comfortable homes? What drives us to do this?" Philip loved to ask the tough questions; he really didn't have an answer that he was dying to give us. He was truly curious about what we thought.

"I come here because you can't find a pub like this anywhere in Minnesota," Mark ventured. "Oh, there are some that come close, but this place has been in business longer than America has had us immigrants in it. I like the people here; I love these pubs; and, I don't know, a little holiday like this just helps me see things differently. But the main thing is that *I like this place*."

"But does it make you see more clearly?"

"I don't know. Isn't enough just to *like* a place?

"Some people travel because they have to," Claire took the floor. "Like me when I was working. Did I enjoy it? Only a few of the perks. I did it because I had to. And what about people who lose their homes like refugees and immigrants? Or how about the homeless? They travel around every day, trying to find a place to eat and sleep. Or, or, what about pilgrims? There've always been pilgrims; I think I might be one, in fact. Not everybody who travels is a tourist."

"Point well taken, my dear. So," Philip was pushing a bit further, "are we tourists or are we mere travelers? Or maybe we're actually vagabonds? Did you ever read George Santayana's essay about the philosophy of travel? In my chefs' school, it was mandatory reading for everyone who wanted to work in the hospitality industry."

I could feel a short lecture starting, and I was wondering when the sandwiches would show up at the table. The lecture came first.

"So, Santayana argued that, whether we're vacationers seeking pleasure or pilgrims seeking meaning, when we travel we're under the watchful eye of Hermes." He looked over and saw a quizzical look on my face. "He's the god of travel. I think we leave what's known and familiar because we're curious about other places and people. Maybe we're here because something is calling us. Santayana argued that when we travel we "take in" people who would otherwise be foreigners to us, and this makes the world smaller and safer."

"Hmmm," I murmured, "I get that. I think something here calls us back time and again. But I thought St Christopher was the patron saint of travelers, so what's with Hermes?"

"That doesn't matter. The point is that there's a force in the universe that seems to push us off our duff, out the door, and to places like this. I mean, here we are, the four of us, sitting in this village pub in a remote part of England, far away from home…"

"…waiting for our lunch," I added just as the proprietor showed up at the table with four sandwiches served with potato salad and, as a surprise, a cup of the soup of the day: a stunning leek and barley soup built on chicken stock, a true Cock-a-Leeky.

"A little gift from the pub for the holidays," she said.

"Well, here's to us," Philip raised his glass, "travelers all."

"And here's to the maker of this soup. Wow. Very kind of them."

"I say, let's toast St Mawgan and this pub. We're away from home—or maybe this *is our home* right now. Let's eat. Cheers!" Leaving aside questions about the philosophy of travel for the moment, we tore into our lunch, chattering away like hens in a farmyard, and enjoying every morsel and drop.

The cock-a-leeky soup was sensational. It's a simple soup: chicken stock flavored with leeks and thickened with barley. On that day in the Falcon, though, it was medicine for us, having come in from a misty, chilly day to this warm and welcoming pub.

Just like we had done a couple of years ago, we wandered over after lunch to visit the monastery and their chickens. As we approached the place, Claire noticed a side door that was standing open. A small, perfectly hand-lettered sign on it read SISTERS' CHAPEL and below that in a smaller font: all are welcome. "You know," Claire said to me, "I always thought I'd be a nun when I was a little girl. Maybe it's not too late." Mark and Philip wandered off with their cameras to capture the poultry on film. Claire and I stepped into the chapel.

We could still smell the incense from that morning's Mass, and the familiar fragrance of freshly extinguished beeswax candles lingered with it. The light broke through a yellow, leaded window creating shapes and angles on the far wall. For the nuns, even though it was December 22nd, Christmas hadn't yet arrived. It was still Advent, so the chapel was wholly unadorned. Christmas for them would begin on December 24th at dusk and run through the Feast of the Epiphany on January 6th—twelve days. They moved at a pace and lived by a calendar which was entirely different from the culture outside their walls.

Claire stepped into one of the pews provided for the public and moved toward the center of it where she sat down. From her perch, she could see every corner of the ancient sanctuary. To her left was a large screen behind which sat the unseen nuns, keeping a constant rotating vigil before the monstrance. To her right was that clutch of windows, shedding their light on the sacred space. I could feel Claire melt into the moment in that chapel; she joined the nuns in their silent prayer, gazing forward, peering into the mystery.

I sat down behind her a couple of rows. I've always loved the smells and bells of chapels like this. I actually shun the large cathedrals in European cities which are crammed with tourists and their cameras and selfie sticks. When I find a space like this one, though, made holy by five hundred years of monks or nuns tending the fires of the world's soul, I can't resist stealing a little of the peace and quiet. I want it to soak in and stay with me.

But since our visit here today came during our journey to St Ives, I glanced at my watch because I knew our cottage would be available at 2 PM and I didn't want to miss a minute of it. I was a teeny bit anxious to get back on the road. We had just enough time to stop here, but I hoped this would be a brief chapel visit.

It wasn't brief. After ten minutes or so, I went outside to see what Mark and Philip were doing. They were busy finding the best angle from which to shoot the old monastery. "Where's Claire?" they asked.

"Well," I told them, "I think she's decided to become a nun. She's still in the chapel." Philip understood this. He went in quietly and sat down beside her, slipping his hand into hers. She purred at his presence but kept her eyes on the sanctuary. He sat patiently by her side; she knew he'd be there as long as she needed.

Mark and I stayed outside in the warm sun. We sat on a bench next to two chickens who had perched beside us. We decided together that this should be the pace of our visit here: We should take as much time as we each needed to absorb whatever the universe was going to give us. No hurry. "We don't need to hurry up and have fun," Mark said. "We really don't have anything we need to do. We can do nothing, and it will be just fine."

International travel can put people on edge: rushing to get there, then waiting once you do arrive, standing in lines, dealing with strangers, using public bathrooms, eating non-food food. It can cause you to be anxious even when being anxious gains you nothing. So, Mark's and my moment there at the Carmelite monastery was an important one. It slowed us down or, in Claire's case, stopped her entirely for a few minutes.

Mark is a painter, oils on canvas, so he knows about working and living at the pace which the painting can bear. There's no such thing as "fast painting." The picture has to present itself to Mark as the artist; it unfolds in front of him slowly and at its own pace. Michelangelo experienced the same thing with a block of marble. The sculpture presented itself slowly as he chipped away what wasn't needed. I'm sure Barbara Hepworth felt the same way. So, as we sat on that chicken bench outside the monastery doors that day, we agreed to let this journey unfold slowly. No need to rush things; no need to push beyond what the experience itself wanted to reveal to us.

Claire decided in the end not to join the convent, and half an hour later, we were back on the A30, driving (more slowly) southwestward toward Hayle. Where the A30 bends south toward Penzance, we joined the A3074 and drove past Carbis Bay into St Ives itself. At Tregenna Place where the B3306 pushes off toward St Just, we turned down the hill into town, past the Golden Lion Pub, swinging left on Market Place and then right on Lifeboat Hill past the parish church and down to the harbor. We found our way through the back streets of the Downalong, coming eventually to our little lane, the Digey, where we stopped the car only long enough to unload it before moving it to a car park some distance away. Many of our temporary, new neighbors were also moving in for the holidays at the same time. The Digey was awash in luggage, bags of holiday décor, and people hustling into their lodgings.

It seemed more and more fitting that we had come to this land of saints to celebrate Christmas. Whether we were saintly or not, we all agreed that associating ourselves with a few good men and women couldn't hurt our chances. We'd just come from St Mawgan and were now in St Ives, just down the road from St. Just.

Chapter 7
The Fisherman's Cottage

The namesake of St Ives was called Ia, a young Irish lass who legend tells us sailed to Cornwall in the mid-5th Century on a leaf, apparently having missed the boat carrying other saints. The Cornish name for the town is *Porthia,* which means, "Port of Ia." Her story is part of the mythology of this place now. We aren't sure why these Irish folks were heading to Cornwall in the first place, but poor, tardy Ia went to the seashore and found that they had gone ahead without her. They may have thought that she was just a child and wouldn't survive the crossing of the stormy Celtic Sea.

No one knows why they left her behind, but, in any case, as saints do, she began to pray. Legend has it that during her prayer, she noticed a leaf floating on the water a small distance out. She touched it with a stick to see if it would sink. Instead of sinking it changed into a small boat into which she gamely climbed and was miraculously carried across the sea. She arrived on the shores of Cornwall in fact before the others. She stayed here and set the stage for this place to become a home to many others, including us tonight.

She was outspoken about the dishonesty and evil she saw around her, especially among the rulers of Cornwall. Eventually, she became a willing martyr for her faith, killed by the evil King Tewdwr Mawr of Penwith. Her loved ones buried her here at what is now St Ives. The parish church stands on her grave.

Tardy saints and willing martyrs aside, we were delighted to be here. As I mentioned, we all eagerly unpacked our luggage and put away our groceries. There were occasional squeals of delight as someone discovered how to light the gas fireplace or where to plug in our music player for the carols. We made a quick decision that we would absolutely and immediately open the bottle of Champagne that our hosts had left for us. We toasted ourselves for having arrived safe and sound. We toasted our cottage for being so charming. We toasted the saints who preceded us here. And, while we were at it, we toasted all things Christmas.

It was December 21st. Even though Mark and I had spent Christmas here in previous years, we left open the planning so that the four of us could decide together how to celebrate the holiday. We each brought our various personal Christmas family traditions with us, compromising on some, dismissing entirely with others, and choosing a way for the four of us that would make us each quite happy. The Christmas holidays can bring out a sense of discontent for folks. People always hope the events of Christmas week will be enough to make them happy, but it doesn't always turn out for everyone. Sometimes families end up fighting, or there's too much of everything and a sort of holiday lethargy exhausts them. For some people, the holidays mean running up credit card debt, trying to provide the ideal celebration—and this creates tension and resentment, which don't lead to happiness. Some people fake happiness to please their mates and are relieved to have it all over at the end of the day.

But we believed that it needn't be that way at all. I suppose that Mark and I had come to St Ives year after year because here we found something more authentic. And the good thing we found is that if we aim mainly to give ourselves to each other instead of to receive gifts at Christmas, then without spending a pound sterling, true happiness does land upon us. We invited friends to join us hoping they, too, would find this more profound joy. We tried to understand this season as a time to renew love, and here, among the rough Cornish miners, the saints, and our fellow holidaymakers, we seemed to find just that. For Claire and Philip, I think, they were on a journey to rediscover each other.

We knew we were taking part in the ancient festival surrounding the winter solstice. On the longest and darkest night of the year— the bleak midwinter—a light shines. Whether it's the dawn at Stonehenge, Yule log fires, the lighting of the Hanukah candle each night on the menorah, midnight Mass, or our own gathering here in the fisherman's cottage in front of our cozy fire, this is a sacred time of year. For the four of us—and we discussed this months ago while planning this journey—it isn't about old traditions as much as about letting this light shine in our hearts—

and, just as importantly, letting it shine between us in the love we share. The activities we planned together were aimed at deeper bonds of friendship.

And so, we made our plans. Tomorrow on the 22nd, we planned that coastal hike and lunch in the village which also ended up leading to the Hepworth museum. We thought we should take some time to just land and get oriented—and a walk along the coast would do the trick.

If the weather was good, we agreed that on the 23rd, we'd head west toward St Just, a small village farther down the peninsula from St Ives. We knew we'd find a great meal at the Tinners Arms in Zennor along the way. Cape Cornwall is near St Just, so we'd also visit there to view the sea and let it blow us around a little. On the evening of that same busy day, we planned to troupe together over to Truro, the county seat of Cornwall. We would visit the cathedral there to attend Lessons and Carols. Afterward, we'd share a simple supper right here at home.

On the 24th, we'd shop. Nothing like putting off the shopping until the last minute, we thought. We were, it is true, trying to escape the commercialism, but we didn't want to give up shopping entirely, and besides, we had decided to share a sweet and simple gift-giving time with each other on Christmas Eve after supper. The kind of shopping one does in St Ives, however, doesn't have anything to do with big box stores and busy parking lots. Instead, it involves serious tea drinking, the eating of scones, some light window shopping, lunch at a local pub with a quaff of beer, at least one nap, more tea, a little more time to shop, and so forth. By 5 PM we would all be exhausted!

On Christmas Day we were planning a sumptuous feast cooked in our kitchen. Mark and I would be in that in charge of that meal. Philip and Claire offered to arrange for the dessert and handle the bar. Together we'd light the fire, tend the music, and put a couple of last-minute touches on our holiday décor. We were cooking our own Christmas dinner in part because we love to cook and in part because most restaurants here are closed on Christmas Day, of which we approve. Mark and I tend to be homebodies anyway, no matter where we are in the world.

We're resistant to the modern trend of eating out a lot; we much prefer to cook in our own kitchen, even if we're renting it. The planning, shopping, sous chefing, and table setting all fit into an art for us: the art of dining. We light candles at home every night, turn down the lights, turn up the torch songs, and linger over dinner—and we've done this for more than two decades. It's our evening event. No television is needed!

We always begin with a toast. I suppose our custom of dining like this is a sort of liturgy for us, vespers and evening Mass all rolled into one. The linens and vessels we use have become sacred to us. The wine is blessed. The bread is homemade. The stories we tell at the table are our very own "scriptures."

But first and foremost: what about tonight's dinner? We all agreed that it seemed like a very long time since our lunch at St Mawgan. 'Oh my,' we asked, 'how could it have been just a few hours earlier?' We were hungry again. It seemed to us that the plan was to eat and drink our way through St Ives. And why not?

We decided that we'd eat later this evening at the Union, our favorite local pub, which gave us time for a cocktail and appetizers here at the house. This also gave us time for the first installment of another agreed part of our plan for the week: reading aloud to each other from a favorite book.

Chapter 8
Moley and Ratty

When we first introduced the idea of reading aloud to Philip and Claire, they seemed reluctant. "You mean from the Internet?" Philip asked. No, we told him, we're going to read an actual book, a hardbound, real book. He rolled his eyes, but slowly warmed to the idea. Claire remembered how her mother had often read to her as a little girl. Philip had to admit that he couldn't remember anyone reading to him, but here we were, so why not? He wanted to be in the "get-along gang," as he put it.

We proposed *The Wind in the Willows* by Kenneth Grahame to them. They had heard of the book but had never read it, and they agreed it would be the one. Mark and I both love this book, and it's an old British favorite, too. Published in 1908, it was still in the top twenty of the current BBC's Big Read survey of all British literature. Pretty good standings for a children's book. We were eager to share it with them and to re-read it ourselves.

Meanwhile, while we were busy discussing the reading plan, Philip was already in the kitchen putting appetizers on plates. "Hey," he hollered to us, "has anyone see the corkscrew? I thought it was right here in the drawer."

"Not me, "I said. I've scarcely been in the kitchen. Mark, have you seen it?"

"Well, where the hell could it be? Did you take it Claire?" It was Philip running out of patience. "These apps are getting cold," he said.

"No, I did not. What would I want with a corkscrew?"

Soon we were all in the kitchen, searching high and low. Finally, someone cracked open the dishwasher in a desperate attempt to look absolutely everywhere, and lo! There it was, sticking in the silverware bin. "Well, who on earth would put a corkscrew in the dishwasher?" he asked.

"Oh, that might have been me," Claire half-whispered, owning up to her crime. "I opened a bottle of sparkling water with the other end of it. I must have put it in there by habit. Sorry."

Then turning to us all she said, "Brace yourselves, guys. It's gonna be a long week. Do you forgive me? You have to forgive me because it's the holidays."

So very soon, candles lit, the fire crackling in front of us, Christmas lights in the windows, a cozy, warm living room in our fisherman's cottage on the Digey in the center of St Ives, glasses of wine all around, we all settled back to read and listen.

One of my earliest memories of childhood in our family farm home was of my mother and sister reading to us from the many "storybooks" we had around the house. Mom was a busy farm wife who had once worked as a teacher, but there was a time in the evenings after we had done the chores and put the supper dishes away, to sit for a spell and read. I fell in love with reading during those early years, and I've never lost that love. It wasn't the text of any one particular book that attracted me as much as that text *read aloud*. Reading aloud brought the stories to life. The characters and contexts of those stories jumped off the page into my young imagination.

When I was in the sixth grade at Perham Public School in my hometown in Minnesota, our teacher, Mrs. Stebbins, read aloud to us every day. Shortly after lunch and before afternoon recess, she would quiet us down and gather us out of our school desks and around her "reading chair" where she sat, holding her book in her lap until we settled down. Then she would begin reading. Everyone became quiet and attentive. She held her book up gracefully and read with a clear, steady voice. Her pastel-colored shawl seemed to become the costume of each character in the stories she read.

She read that year from three novels, but *Anne of Green Gables* was the first. We all felt we knew Anne, Gilbert, and Diana Barry, Anne's bosom friend. The story was about perseverance, flexibility, kindness, and pluck. In the story, Anne was mistakenly sent by an orphanage to live with unmarried siblings Marilla and Matthew Cuthbert who were in their fifties. They had asked the orphanage to send a boy to help with farm chores at Green Gables, but Anne showed up instead. What sixth-grade child hasn't felt that maybe he or she was dropped into their family accidentally by some outside force, as 11-year-old Anne had been?

Initially made unwelcome by Marilla, the Cuthberts did finally take her in, and the story unfolds as she makes friends, attends school, and establishes her life there. Each of us in our class listened as Mrs. Stebbins (who quite possibly never had a first name) spun each day's yarn. Our little imaginations created the house, the schoolyard, and the small town in which they all lived. We saw the faces of her friends and the two people who were her foster parents. It was as real to us as the paper I'm writing on now. This shared, wild, imaginative story has never left me.

I know there was eventually a movie made from this book, but I refused to ever go see it. I felt the same way about the Dickens novels or even Victor Hugo. Seeing someone else's idea of the details in these stories would rob me of my own vivid memories of them. Too much media blunts one's imagination, I think.

Reading aloud as adults is an intimate and profoundly delightful way to spend time. In my prep school, we studied Latin in every term. In our fourth year, we translated the first six books of the Aeneid into English. It was hard work, but the most pleasurable part of the task was that we read nearly the entire epic poem aloud to each other in the classroom. Even though it was in Latin, something about the flow of the dactylic hexameter with its occasional couplets was far more immediate than merely reading it silently to ourselves would have been.

Monks and nuns used to eat their meals in silence while listening to scripture or spiritual literature. And among the last places these days where someone reads aloud to a crowd is in churches and synagogues. There a lector proclaims the various scripture readings. Everyone else sits and listens. Church leaders could merely pass out the texts and let everyone read them on their own, but something powerful happens when we listen together. Reading aloud draws us toward each other, and the meaning of the readings becomes more real.

When someone reads aloud to us, the words wash over us like a gentle rain. We hear the same words of prose or poetry that we would read silently to ourselves, but the story opens up as we hear the sentences and paragraphs. When we listen to stories, we imagine the characters more vividly in our mind's eye than ever could happen with a movie; and the details of the story—the weather, the experience of each character, the sound of the wind or the river—are more tangible and audible. It's a wholly different experience than reading to ourselves or even listening to an audiobook.

"So why not?" we said to each other. We had considered Dickens' *A Christmas Carol* or maybe Dylan Thomas' *A Child's Christmas in Wales*, but we landed instead on the story of Moley and Ratty and their friends along the Riverbank and in the Wild Wood: Otter, Badger, and Mr. Toad. We read in turns, passing the book around the room, each reading a couple of pages before handing the book along to the next.

The story begins with Mole. He's down in his underground home, and he's doing something we've all had to do: spring cleaning. He's wiping away the winter cobwebs, sweeping the floors, and cleaning out the fireplace. But while doing the chore he disliked the most—the messy and difficult job of whitewashing the walls—he quite suddenly threw down his brooms and mops and escaped into the bright spring sunlight above. Oh my, what a great experience it is to leave behind the claustrophobic darkness and emerge into the wide-open space of a sunlit savannah. We all bear within us the memory of having done that, or the desire to do it soon. And isn't that precisely what Claire was in the process of doing? She had thrown off the shackles of her corporate job and was only now breathing in the fresh air and sunlight she needs.

The Mole was free at last! He rambled alone at first across pastures and fields, observing everything as if for the first time. What a glorious feeling it is to see everything anew. Such a new seeing is part of what we hope going on holiday might bring us. To answer the question that Philip posed in the Falcon about why we were all there in St Ives, away from our homes, here is part of the answer. Like the Mole, we go on holiday in the hope that we might see anew and become more curious about the world around us. Bill Bryson once remarked on this—and I can't recall where he said this— "I can't think of anything that excites a great sense of childlike wonder than to be in a country where you are ignorant of almost everything."

It's that sense of wonder: seeing everything with excitement and curiosity that is so much a part of being on holiday. That's what Mole was experiencing as he roamed along the hedgerows. And it's precisely what Mark and I experience each and every time we're in England and St Ives.

Finally, the Mole reached the Riverbank. He found it fascinating, a word that indeed describes what it's like to be entranced by something. It comes from the original Latin word *fascinum*, which means, literally, to be put under a spell or into a trance. The Mole walked briskly alongside the river for a while, mesmerized by the sounds, the spray, and the color of the water. He couldn't pull himself away; indeed, the river put a spell on him and captured him.

I think that explains why Mark and I keep coming back to St Ives. It has us under a spell, and we are fascinated. St Ives is full of stories, just like the river was for Mole that day. The river chattered to him, spilling out the great stories of the world, all following the river as it leads down to the sea.

Indeed, the very best stories in the world. As we read to each other—and listened, too— there in our cottage, spilling out this lovely story, an excitement emerged among us. We felt ourselves being drawn into the experiences of the characters. We nibbled our appetizers and sipped our wine while the story filled the room and our imaginations like a vast cloud of incense from the bottle of a genie. The story was romantic and entrancing for us.

We all loved this story as it unfolded but, of course, we hadn't just flown eight hours and driven another four to sit here in our cottage and read. So, after a while, appetizers notwithstanding, our plucky hunger got the best of us, and I suggested we should probably head out for our supper at the Union Inn.

"Oh, but I wanna see where the Mole ends up," Claire begged. "Let's just read a little more."

"Are we close to this Union pub?" Philip asked.

"About a five-minute walk."

Mark and I knew the story because we had read this book several times before, but Claire and Philip were hanging on each line. In a way, they were under the spell of this book now, so we agreed to find a stopping point a little further along in the story. We read onward.

As the Mole sat along the riverbank watching the local residents go about their days, the story told us, he saw various animals trudging here and there. One was building a new spring nest in this tree. Another was digging a new spring home along that hedgerow. As he sat there, Mole realized that he wasn't feeling any guilt about not whitewashing his walls. His conscience was not pricking him. Quite the contrary, he thought it was very jolly to be idle while everyone else was working. Ah yes, another reason to enjoy travel when you're on holiday—or even just when you're loafing.

At this point, an incident occurred in the story that became the turning point for Mole. He was sitting idly on the edge of the river and gazing across it. Every time I read this story, I am struck by the fact that Mr. Mole was doing, literally, *nothing*. He was just sitting there as I do in my favorite spot in St Paul. We must remember that he was still under its spell and he was entranced. Suddenly, his eye caught a dark hole about halfway up the bank on the opposite side of the river. He thought to himself that such a natural den would make a snug little home for an animal with few cares. But as he looked, he thought he saw—no it couldn't have been—but yes, something did twinkle down in the heart of the hole and then just as quickly vanish. Intrigued now, the Mole leaned in and looked more closely. Whatever or whoever was in there positively twinkled again. He knew it couldn't be a star. But what was it? He decided then and there that it was an eye. The eye of some animal. And sure enough, a face emerged, a brown face with whiskers. It was the Water Rat! The face of this creature appeared in full light, and they regarded each other momentarily across the river.

"Hello, Mole," said the Rat cautiously.

"Hello, Rat."

Claire giggled as she read this section. The idea of these two animals eyeing each other and then calling each other by name across the river seemed preposterous to her, and she said so. "It's ridiculous," she said.

"Oh, I don't know, Honey," Philip turned to face her even though they were cuddling on the couch. "This is how we met."

"It is not."

"It is so. You've forgotten. Your law firm sent you to Sam and Sylvia's house, to that fundraiser for Paul Wellstone. Remember that?"

"Well, I certainly didn't stare at you across the room like some googling idiot."

"I thought you did. You had your eye on me all evening, am I right?"

"I suppose maybe I noticed you. A little."

"And you finally said hello. Just like the Rat said to the Mole."

"Will you two please settle this later up in your room?" I said. "We're never going to get to supper if you two can't get along. Anyway, I know Philip is right, Claire. I've heard this damn story a dozen times. Gimme the book."

She handed it over, and I continued. Sure enough, the two animals agreed to meet. "Sound familiar?" Philip sang to Claire. She stuck out her tongue at him. In any case, in the story, the Rat loosened the ties on his boat, a small blue boat with a white interior, and sculled smartly across the river. Then he held up his forepaw and helped the Mole step into the boat.

"Ahhh. How sweet is that?" Philip was really enjoying this. "Just like me on our second date when I helped you at that wedding. Remember?" Claire nodded, and we could all see she was letting Philip know that he was right. Philip and Claire, just like Moley and Ratty, had become friends immediately after they met. Their friendship has helped them through thick and thin. "This has been a wonderful day," the Mole said as the Rat shoved off from the bank. "Oh Sweetie, haven't we had a wonderful life?"

There was a pause then while Mark popped out to the kitchen for more wine. I went with him, giving our two friends a minute alone. It was only a little after 6 PM, but it felt later because all our internal clocks were off. Mark and I agreed together that we should read ahead to the end of this chapter before supper. We had plenty of time, so we returned to the story.

The Mole loved the boat, but he confessed to the Rat that this was his first experience on the water. The Rat was astonished! He was nearly speechless. He was a water rat who lived on the river and from the river. It was his whole life. It seemed incomprehensible to him that anyone would not know about the river. And this blind spot on the part of the Rat, assuming that everyone else shared his river culture, was yet another reason to explore a new place, meet new people, experience new foods, and learn what life is like for people we don't know.

The Rat was determined to share his experience with his new companion. He turned to the inexperienced Mole and said, "Believe me, my young friend, there is NOTHING—absolutely nothing—half so much worth doing as simply messing about in boats." Indeed, the Mole would eventually have to come to that appreciation himself. Later that day, according to the story, they rowed Ratty's boat up the river with a large basket full of cold chicken, salads, French rolls, gherkins, ginger beer, and lemonade. They were planning a picnic, and the Rat was slowly introducing the Mole to what living on the river was like. Mole was ecstatic about it.

The two friends found a peaceful spot for their picnic on a green part of the riverbank. Otter joined them and, for a brief moment—a very brief moment—the Badger also appeared but, being a solitary creature, quickly returned to the safety of the forest. The afternoon was drawing to a close when they packed up the leftovers and headed to the boat once again. On the way back down the river, the Mole got it into his head that he should be allowed to row. The Rat protested, pointing out that Mole was new to all this and might not be quite ready. But as they lazily floated along, the Mole, without waiting for instructions of any kind, grabbed the oars and gave a considerable pull. He managed to overturn the boat in the cold water, spilling the two animals as well as their lunch basket into the river.

"Well that goofy Mole," I said. "He should have known better."

"Famous last words from the guy who never learned to swim," Mark said. "How many times have I had to save you?"

"Countless, I know." It was true. Mark had saved me in ways I didn't even know I needed saving. Not so much from drowning in a river as from drowning in my own oddities and quirks.

And in the story, Mole's patient new friend put everything right again—the boat, the lunch basket, and the Mole himself—and then the Rat hauled his wet friend to his own home along the riverbank. There the Rat built a warm and roaring fire in the living room, sat the Mole down in a comfortable armchair, gave him a dressing gown and slippers, and then joined him. Ratty then proceeded to tell Mole river stories until suppertime. How darned sweet.

As Claire read when it was her turn, she sat upright and held the book aloft in front of her, looking very much like Mrs. Stebbins, her reading glasses perched on her nose. Her shawl lay across her shoulders in just the same way. I closed my eyes and was transported back to the 6ᵗʰ grade. There I was, eleven years old and journeying down the river with Moley and Ratty. 'In this part of the story,' I thought to myself, 'Mark is right. I am much more like the Mole: naïve, impetuous, eager, and wowed by everything. Sweet Mark was the steady Rat: packing the lunch, steering the boat, and saving us in the end from the disasters that I instigated.'

And at this wonderful point in the story, we left the new friends for the time being. Supper was calling us. As I have already said, if you could count on anything among the four of us, it was our appetites. We put away the book, put out the candles, and in something of a mad rush, made for the door all at once.

The entry hall of our cottage also doubled as our "coat closet" with a single rail and six or eight coat hooks on it. Umbrellas leaned in the corner and boots stood on the floor. It was unlit and just wide enough for one person at a time, but somehow, we four managed to squeeze ourselves crazily into this tiny space as we got ready to leave. We were all only half ready when we flung open the door and suddenly realized that we had to bundle up a bit more. There was a rainy chill in the air in St Ives. So, we all tumbled back in, closed the door, and started over. A bit of hilarity ensued as we dressed each other, wrapping scarves and pulling down our hats, and finally, we left in better order, one at a time.

The Digey was not six feet wide. Not so much a street as a granite-cobbled alley. We tumbled out our doorway and down our very narrow and uneven stair. At the bottom, we gathered ourselves, making room for passersby and neighbors to come and go while we got our troupe assembled. There was Christmas cheer in the air among everyone we met. "Happy Christmas," they would say, and we echoed it back just the same. Happy Christmas everyone.

Chapter 9
The Union Inn & Stargazy Pie

It was raining that night but after all that folderol in our doorway as we left, at least we had our umbrellas this evening. As we all negotiated the six steep stairs from our door down to the Digey, we turned left and headed to Fore Street and the center of town. We were finally on our way to the Union Inn. Mark and I have been in this pub so often over the years that, when we enter now, we half expect someone to holler out our names and slap us on the back. To the left inside is a warm fire with couches and tables and dogs all around it. To the right is the bar which is also surrounded by pub tables. There is a room in the back as well, and it's often full, especially during the holidays. People are playing cards, leaning in to hear intimate conversations, meeting neighbors, and enjoying a pint.

We found a table for four, ordered pints of beer and cider, and settled in to look at the menu. The Union offers authentic pub fare: fish and chips, cottage pie, bubble & squeak, sausage and mash, fish pie, and a dozen other lovely dishes. It wasn't hard to choose because we knew we'd be back, so if we didn't order it on this visit, there would always be a "next time." Always. The Union is our "home pub" in St Ives where we can always go and where there is always a welcome.

Not that long ago the pubs in England were the butt of jokes about cuisine. They were dark and murky places, dense with the haze of smoke from cigarettes and cigars. Today, though, a lot of local pubs have excellent kitchens, professional chefs, and great menus. They've earned the name, gastropubs. There is no smoking in these pubs any longer and, amazingly, everyone obeys that new rule. They're bright and cheery now without having lost their woody, comfortable charm.

Whenever we arrive at a pub like this one, we feel excited and eager. We never know what new experience awaits us. As in most pubs, at the Union, orders are placed at the bar. There really aren't any waiters. When the food is ready, someone from the kitchen will deliver it to your table, but otherwise, people are expected to serve themselves. So we huddled around our table and made our meal choices for tonight, put in our order at the bar for both food and drink, carried our various pints to the table, and promptly pulled out a deck of cards to play a few hands of Hearts.

Hearts is a card game where the goal is to not earn points. You really don't want to take tricks—any tricks whatsoever—unless you have such good cards that you can take all the tricks, which gives all the other players a lot of points that they don't want. One earns these unwanted points either by taking a heart in a trick for one point each or by taking the queen of spades for thirteen ugly points. While we waited for our meal, we played a couple of hands amid much protesting by whoever landed the queen. I must say that Claire, for all her professional smarts, did not seem to understand the whole queen thing. It actually seemed at one point as though she was *trying* to take the queen on the principle that any monarchist would want to have a Queen.

For the people sitting at the tables near us, this all seemed quite strange. A fellow at one of those tables kept an eye on us for a few hands, and then this whole odd strategy of trying not to take tricks got the best of him, and he had to ask how this game worked. "To win, you have to lose," one of us explained. "We're trying very hard not to take any tricks."

"Oh sure. Uh-huh." A long pause. "Are you Canadians?" he asked. Gratefully at that moment, the food arrived.

I have a weakness for shepherd's pie, and tonight's dish was outstanding as always. The chef had braised the lamb and added onion, carrot, garlic, and celery. Then he finished it with a red wine reduction. The herbs were thyme and bay, very subtle and savory. He topped it with mashed potatoes that he seasoned with cheddar and nutmeg. Just delicious.

The catch of the day was plaice, a right-eyed flounder which is common in England and much of Europe. It had Mark's name on it. The chef prepared it Meuniere style, meaning in lemon and butter. He used flavorful Cornish butter, no doubt from local and happy cows. He served it with mushy peas and new potatoes. I'm telling you, it was sensational. Here in this old, local pub at the edge of England, the chef was superb.

Not everyone loves mushy peas. They're marrowfat peas (peas which have been left in the field to dry naturally), and they start out life much harder than the usual table variety of green pea. Once harvested, they're soaked overnight in water and baking soda. Then they're rinsed in fresh water and simmered with a little sugar (they can be bitter). In time, they'll form a thick green mash. They often have a green-grey sort of color which is not appetizing to everyone, but many times food color is added to make them a brighter green. Sometimes mint is added to flavor them a bit. They're very popular in the North, but these days they're served throughout England.

In one of our pubs back home, which purports to be authentically English (really, how can it be?) they substituted coleslaw for mushy peas on their fish and chips last summer. We protested and stopped eating the fish and chips until they returned the mushy peas to the plate. So, I guess you'd have to say that we have acquired a taste for them.

It seemed we might not have a meal together without someone ordering the mussels and tonight it was Claire. They were exceptional. Often considered a Belgian or French dish, a pot of west country Cornish Moules Mariniere is supper at its best. Mussels require only fresh, inexpensive ingredients, but they always seem celebratory. The menu said that the chef would prepare these in "the traditional way" with garlic, white wine, and cream, but the chef also added a healthy dose of leeks to the broth—leeks are, after all, in season here in December—deepening the savory flavors. Like in Belgium, they were served with hand-cut chips. The beautiful thing about a dish of mussels is that, when you finish with them, you have the delicious wine and garlic sauce left in which to dip chunks of bread. It's a feast! We ordered a second basket of bread and devoured it.

Philip had hoped we might find stargazy pie on the menu, but we were a few miles off. Stargazy pie is indeed a Cornish dish made of whole baked pilchards—sometimes called sardines—often cooked in a creamy gravy with potatoes, and covered with a pastry crust. What sets this dish apart from other fish pies is the somewhat unsettling fact that its leading feature is fish heads—and sometimes tails—protruding through the crust! They're situated so that they seem to be gazing at the stars, hence the name. They say that this allows the oils released during cooking to flow back into the pie, but I don't know; I hate to face my lunch before eating it.

Stargazy pie seems to have originated from the village of Mousehole (pronounced mowz-ull) which is on the other side of the peninsula, next door to Penzance. Mousehole is worth the journey across Cornwall. Their harbor is picturesque and ringed with pubs and shops. On Christmas Eve itself, the town throws a sort of harbor party complete with chestnuts roasting on open fires, yuletide carols, and yes, folks dressed up like, well, like an English version of an Eskimo. We found our way over there one year, managed to park the car, which was truly miraculous, and we were there for that annual magical moment when, at dusk, the Mayor of Mousehole flips the switch and all the boats, as well as the harbor itself, were flooded with holiday lights. It was sensational.

In any case, there would be no stargazy pie for Philip tonight at the Union Inn, so instead, he tried their famous Steak and Doombar Ale pie with mash. This ale and the pie derived from it are named after a bar of sand which lies at the mouth of the River Camel, just where it meets the Celtic Sea on the north coast of Cornwall. The sands have often shifted during storms, and many sailors have lost their lives there, hence its dark and gloomy name: doombar.

The making of a good steak and ale pie requires half a day of simmering and cooling before a puff pastry crust is added to top it off. The chef here dredged the beef in flour, salt, what seems like too much black pepper, and thyme. He sautéed the carrots, onions, and garlic until they were tender. Then he cooked the dredged beef in the vegetables. He poured in a big draft of Sharp's Doombar, a Cornish ale with lots of character. He added peas and a generous number of mushrooms, and then he let the mixture sit and simmer for a couple of hours. He likes to chill the pie mixture for a while or even overnight to let the flavors mingle. The chef then poured the pie filling into individual crocks, covered it with the puff pastry, added some slits to allow it to blow off steam during the baking, and popped it into the oven for about forty minutes. Voila!

The dining got underway with a lot of enthusiasm on our parts. But first, there would be some toasts. "To my dear Claire," Philip began, "to her queenly insanity." Claire purred her approval, and it was starting to become clear that she was on her way "home" to Philip.

"To the sheep, God bless 'em, who gave his life for my pie."

"To all our friends back home tonight. It's snowing in Minnesota, and aren't we glad to be here?"

"And aren't we lucky to have this food? Really, so lucky. Here's to us all."

The English poet John Milton once wrote that gratitude "bestows reverence, allowing us to encounter everyday epiphanies," and perhaps that's why gratitude is part of every toast and blessing. Vacation travel can become very self-indulgent, a time when we allow ourselves to wallow in the pleasures of food and drink, forgetting that what we have comes from good fortune. But when we pause, even during vacation, to recognize our luck, what might have been just another meal on the road becomes a transcendent moment of awe. Such moments can "change forever how we experience life and the world," Milton wrote.

As we sit down to eat, I often think of the people around the world who will have no meal today, no ability to feed their own children. I have worked no harder than them. I'm not any smarter than most people. But I have had extraordinary luck to have been born and raised in a place that fostered me. This lovely supper at the Union Inn is only a celebration when we remember this with gratitude. We must also allow the gratitude to motivate us to work for greater equity and a fairer distribution of these things. This is the reverence that Milton wrote about in the 1600s. It isn't so much a religious sentiment as it is a thoroughly human one.

We chatted about all this while we lingered at the table after our meal. We had switched at some point in the evening from pints of ale to glasses of wine, which they serve on tap at the Union. But soon, plates wiped clean and wine glasses empty, we were all sleepy and ready to head home. It was hard to believe that we had only arrived in Cornwall and St Ives that afternoon. We'd driven that day from up near Bristol south to Exeter, swinging around to the west on the A30 and down the peninsula with a side trip to St Mawgan for lunch and "midday prayers" at the convent. From there we journeyed onward to St Ives. Tomorrow we were planning an early coastal walk out toward Zennor. We had unpacked, consulted our maps, shared a pre-prandial, and helped Claire understand that darn queen of hearts. This first day was drawing to a close now.

We strolled back to our fisherman's cottage, savoring the smells and tastes and sounds of the Union, saying that we were just like the Mole and the Rat, enjoying that picnic lunch they had on the river today. There were still a few folks bustling around town, but the Digey was quiet as we made our way back to the warm cottage for our first night's sleep.

We each went to bed quickly and quietly, but Mark brought a small tray of Port and two glasses to our room. We lit a candle and turned off the light, laying there together propped up on our pillows, sipping the Port and talking about our day, about Claire and Philip, about unwinding from the usual busyness around us. We laid awake listening to the final party-goers of the night heading home along the Digey which was below our windows. Soon, though, we were sleepy. We had an exciting day planned for tomorrow, and we had traveled many miles today. We fell asleep as Christmas dreams danced in our heads.

Chapter 10
Cape Cornwall and the Tinners Arms

The whole of the UK is about the size of our home state of Minnesota, some ninety-thousand square miles. Cornwall is a mere 1376 square miles, about eighty miles long and forty-five miles wide, but many parts of the peninsula are much narrower than that. This size makes it possible to drive from one end of the county to the other rather quickly by our standards. For local people, however, a trip to, say, Truro, some twenty-six miles from St Ives, may involve long conversations to plan, choose the route, and pack the car.

Cornwall is a county in England, but part of the Duchy of Cornwall is also located here. The Duchy includes land in several counties, including Herefordshire, Devon, Isles of Scilly, and Somerset. So, the *Duchy* of Cornwall, which comprises some two-hundred square miles of land in several locations scattered throughout this area, is not the same as the *County* of Cornwall. We find this fact, frankly, to be very confusing. This Duchy, though, was established a long time ago, in 1337, by King Edward III for his heir and son, Prince Edward. At that time, the rule was that each future Duke of Cornwall would be the eldest surviving son of the King or Queen and the heir to the throne. Today, however, daughters can also be named Duke—or would that be Duchess?

At any rate, at this writing, the Duke of Cornwall is Charles, Prince of Wales. The Duke has a role to play in local life. He appoints the sheriff, profits from the ports, and manages the lands. Naturally, in these modern times, there is a movement to end the whole Duchy system and turn over its land holdings to the public. But as we see it, one of the functional outcomes of having the Duchy is that it offers a layer of protection from would-be "developers." To get a permit here to change the countryside, one must pass through a gauntlet of hurdles and officials. Because of that, the hedgerows, fences, and even old gates in the countryside rarely move or change. Old buildings don't get torn down. Big box stores rarely get a permit to build. There's a strong public will to preserve the culture by making change slowly, or maybe not at all in many cases. We like that. It's one of the reasons this place has retained its charm.

At any rate, duchies and counties aside, our plan for the day was to visit the western end of the peninsula, so we drove out of St Ives on the B3306 past Zennor and onward to Cape Cornwall, a fifteen-mile but the forty-five-minute journey. On the winding, one-lane road leading westward, we passed between those unchanged hedgerows which crowded the road on either side. These lanes were all lined with gorse and heather. This was a road built for horses but not for cars. We drove by nearly a dozen small points whose names read like an ancient travelogue: Treen, Porthmeor, Morvah, Bojewyan, Pendeen, Trewellard, Carnyorth, Botallack, Kenidjack. Off to the right as we passed Trewellard we could see the Levant and Geevor tin mines, their lonely chimneys and riggings now stark against the horizon of the sea. Along the way, stone farm buildings and an occasional inn suggested that this place was not as isolated as it seemed. Fields of sheep flanked the road or were sometimes *on the road*; those old gates and hedgerows covered the landscape, and we felt as though we were driving back in time.

This Cornish peninsula forms the tip of the very southwestern-most point of England. Everything west of here is the Atlantic Ocean, all the way past the Isles of Scilly and onward to St John's Newfoundland and North America. On our first visit, we noticed that the whole area had a surprisingly mild and warm climate; we know now that it is regulated by the Gulf Stream, bringing in warm currents of water. There are small-sized palm trees in the area along with a vibrant, tropical-looking plant cover. On Cornwall's moors—and this end of the peninsula is covered by moors—the high elevation makes tree cover impossible because of the wind, so instead there is a dense ground cover of shrubs and bushes. It all feels untamed and wild.

As we drove westward, we slowly became aware that the winds were picking up speed quickly. The light mists we had noticed in St Ives had become a bit steadier by the time we arrived here. We'd been running the wipers now and then; it wasn't quite raining but certainly not dry. We decided that we'd work up our appetite for lunch by visiting the Cape first, just in case the weather worsened. Cape Cornwall can be wild and woolly on a calm day because it's so fully exposed to the sea and the winds so we thought we'd better take advantage of this light mist and consider it as good as we'd get for that day. Anyway, lunch wouldn't be available in the pubs until after midday, so off to the Cape we went.

This is the only cape in England—a cape being a point of land where two bodies of water meet. It's at this point that the English Channel, the busiest shipping area of the world, meets the Celtic Sea and the Atlantic Ocean. On the north side, the Bristol Channel takes ships all the way inland to Cardiff and Bristol. On the south side, the Channel separates England from France. For a long time, this Cape was thought to be the westernmost point of all England, but recent ordinance surveys have determined that it's Land's End which holds that honor, just a few miles south along the coast. Be that as it may, when you stand on the Cape, with its headlands and stormy seas, it *feels* much wilder and out-there than the more commercial Land's End does.

We pulled into the car park at Cape Cornwall at about 11 AM. We slowed to a stop just inside the gate, peering out the car windows, thinking maybe we were in the wrong place. While it was a car park built for fifty or seventy-five cars, there were only two others there. Where was everybody? We surveyed what stretched out before us down toward the sea and realized that maybe so few people were there because it was very, very windy. Gale winds. It turned out they were blowing at forty-three knots, which we liked to say even though none of us fully understood what that meant. We learned the term from a local coast watch volunteer; it means the winds were at about fifty miles per hour.

We'd been talking in the car about the Heinz family. Yes, H.J. Heinz, the ketchup and pickle people. It turns out that they had bought this entire area as an old tin mine and donated the whole thing to the National Trust of England to commemorate a century of British business in the baked bean and ketchup trade. The National Trust here is marvelous. It has the mission of preserving and opening to the public many monumental gardens, buildings, and sites. It relies on a large contingent of volunteers at every location who are always friendly and helpful. In any case, this whole Cape is now under their trust.

A tin mine had been opened here in 1838. There was a mining boom going on in Cornwall then, but this was a small and somewhat unprofitable mine. The owners depended heavily on cheap labor from women and children to operate—the mine shafts they had to crawl through were tiny. In 1864, the St Just Consolidated Mines built the tall chimney that still stands on the peak of the Cape. Over the years the mine was opened and closed several times, but the final blow came from the Metalliferous

Mines Regulation Act of 1872 and the Factory and Workshop Act of 1878 which, taken together, drastically limited the use of low-cost female and child labor.

We pulled to a stop and started sorting out our gear for the hike to the top of the Cape. Claire meanwhile had that huge, unfolded map of hers out and fully open. She was tracing our progress down the narrow road and reporting on it to us from the back seat. It was quite helpful. But once we decided that we were in the right place and that we were going to stay, both Philip and Claire opened their back doors at the same time to get out. When they did this an unexpectantly massive blast of wind came whipping through the car with such force that it grabbed Claire's map and blew it halfway across the empty parking lot. She shrieked and, in a moment's rush, she jumped out of the car and went dashing after it, scarf blowing, coat unbuttoned, arms and legs all flying at once. In her dash, she managed to step right into a deep puddle of water before she grabbed her map and dashed back to the car, jumping in and slamming the door. In the moment's silence that followed, no one dared laugh. Then all at once, including her. "Oh. My. Goodness," she said. "It is wet and wild out there."

She was correct. There was definitely rain, but the wind made it looked wetter than it really was. Besides, this was England—it rains a lot here. One really can't let the weather deter one's plans, we have always said. "Well, what do you think?" someone asked. For a moment or two, we sat quietly staring out at what had become a very stormy morning, but nobody wanted to be the one who pulled the plug on this adventure. "Well, for Pete's sake," Mark finally said. "We came all this way; we aren't going home without seeing the Cape, are we?"

And then the planning got underway in earnest. We hadn't dressed for this much weather. We had one umbrella in the car, but it would never have stood up to these winds. We'd all have to bundle up a bit more. I wrapped an extra scarf I had around my hat and wound it down around my neck and tucked it into my tweed jacket; it wasn't much, but it would have to do. Philip suggested that Claire could use his backpack if he emptied it. She looked at him like he was crazy but then said, "Give it to me." She took it and put it over her head, upside down, straps to the back. It was a sight, but it would keep her dry. "Well, I'm officially a bag lady," she said. Mark, the only sensible one in our group, was wearing a very long rain slicker with a hood which he pulled up over his head and tied tightly. All you could see were his eyes peeking out from the zippered raincoat. Philip was ready to accept the fact that he was going to be soaked, but then we found a plastic grocery sack which we had been using in the car as a garbage bag. He emptied the refuse, pulled it over his hat, and tied it to his scarf under his chin. He looked like a babushka, but at least he would keep dry.

And we set off gamely for the Cape. One by one this time, we opened the car doors and slipped out into the wind. It immediately puffed out whatever we had on and the four of us: backpack head, scarf head, bag head, and slicker head, set out carefully, staying close together. We looked like a tribe of Bedouins in our strange headgear. We walked down the hill from the car park, through the gate, and alongside the old mining offices which we assumed were now holiday lodging, although I don't think anyone was at home that day. The sea was full of power, pounding on the rocks in front of us as the rain came down. Looking out over the edge at Priests' Cove down below, it was forty feet down to the water, but the spray of the surf easily reached us on every crashing wave. It was absolutely mad and spectacular! None of us had ever seen the sea like this.

We tried to talk, but the wind blew our voices away. At one point, Philip was saying something to us—I'm sure it was about how much fun this was—but his words along with some spittle just flew out of his mouth and on toward the sea.

At the bottom of the Cape was a handmade stair which wound around the point to the right. We stopped and double-checked our various bits of headgear. It was all holding, so we made our way slowly around to the right and up the stair along the edge of the sea. The winds subsided a little as we moved behind the hill. Up and up we went along the seawall, up over the huge rocks, and up very high where we found another stairway with a railing that led to the National Coastwatch lookout station which was at the top. We paused before heading up that stair to look out over the sea. We could see through the mist to the Brisons, a twin-peaked islet offshore that was said to resemble Charles de Gaulle lying on his back. We agreed we'd have to come back on a brighter day to double-check that. Charles de Gaulle? Really?

Anyway, we made our way up the final stair to the lookout station and were delighted to find a welcome sign on the door and a note that invited everyone inside. Into the small building we trudged. There we found Nigel, the volunteer watchman on duty that day. He took one look at us, and I think he regretted the welcome sign. We must have been a sight! But his station, small and cozy, was also warm and dry, which we needed just then. We slipped off our headgear, which at least gave us the appearance of being normal.

There are fifty of these watch stations crewed by over two-thousand volunteers keeping watch around the British Isles from Rossall Point in the Northwest, through Wales, to Wearside in the Northeast along the southern coast all the way to this one in remote Cornwall. Great Britain is an island, after all—actually, it's an archipelago of islands, one-hundred-eight-seven inhabited islands in Great Britain, in addition to a couple of thousand uninhabited ones—and islands are by definition surrounded by water. In England's case, the water is the rough and wooly North Sea, the Atlantic Ocean, and the stormy Celtic Sea. And the island is beset with rocky coastlines and busy, challenging shipping lanes.

Of course, ships do use exceptionally sophisticated technology these days, but a computer can't spot a distress flare from an amateur yachtsman or professional fisherman in trouble. These volunteers are the eyes and ears along the coast, watching the charts, monitoring radio channels, and listening for problems when there is inadequate visibility. Nigel was eager to explain it all to us, including the bit about knots versus miles per hour. We took turns looking out through his telescope and, even on this stormy day, we could see ships moving in and out of the channel on his radar.

Finally, we bundled ourselves back up for the descent and left Nigel, feeling like we'd traversed the storm to reach him. One by one we filed out, headgear all secure, ready for the arduous climb down. But on our way down the first stairway, a small family came bounding up, both parents with bare heads and three kids playing like it was not a dark and stormy day.

"They're all going to get pneumonia," Claire said under her breath.

"Jeez," I said. "When did I get to be such an old guy?"

"How do you think that mom will explain a woman with a backpack stuck on her head?" Philip mused.

As is always the case, the descent seemed to go much more quickly than the ascent had, but the wind and the rain were picking up steam, so we promptly headed to the carpark without lollygagging very much.

Once back securely in the car and heading to Zennor for our lunch, we all agreed that this is a lovely, lovely place. The power and beauty of the surf so moved us that it was tough to leave, weather conditions notwithstanding. Our hike had led us past old tin mines, up along a seawall beside wild and crashing waves, and onto the dark and dangerous cliffs at the top. Heathcliff, eat your heart out. Wonderfully clean and clear air surrounded us—and nearly blew us over— and the light had the color of an azure haze. How heavenly it would have been to fall asleep for an afternoon nap to the sound of the sea in some nearby bed and breakfast.

But there would be no naps for us. Lunch was in the air, and the Tinners Arms was our destination, yet another favorite pub of ours. How many favorites can there be? We made our way down the one-lane road back to Zennor—it's only a few miles—and parked in the small lot beside the pub. The Tinners Arms has a small door leading directly into the bar. Inside to the right is a massive fireplace with a cozy log fire. The bar is to the left, and it's where people and their dogs tend to hang. Ancient pub tables fill the rest of the room. A second dining room is also available and, in good weather, the outside patio. The place is always busy.

101

We dashed through the storm and tumbled into the pub door, finding to our delight that the table next to the log fire had just opened up. We put Claire and her wet foot next to the fire and the rest of us around the table. This pub had been built in 1271. To us that seemed very, very old. The people of this village have had the benefit of it for over seven-hundred years. It was originally built to house the masons who constructed St Senara's—the local parish church. Very little here seems to have changed over the years, and all the cares and troubles of modern life slip away as you step inside this homey pub.

The Tinners Arms might be one of the most dog-friendly pubs in England. We love that the pubs welcome well-mannered dogs. They tend to stay close to their owners or to find a napping spot while the human party goes on. Today was no exception. The presence of these canines adds to the warm comfort of the place. They have in some pubs—and I am not making this up—what they call an "alaBark menu" for the dogs. Yes, you can actually order lunch for your dog.

The managers and staff of this pub are always tending their regulars and welcoming newcomers. Owners Anna and James George have a chef who knows his way around the kitchen. So, as someone added more logs to the fire and took our orders, the chef went to work. Other patrons were already wiping their chins and pushing back their chairs while new lunch seekers came rushing in out of the wind and rain, which we had by this time all but forgotten was going on outside. We were ready for something to eat. This pub, like many others these days, has a great kitchen. We've never had a bad meal here.

We decided in the car to forego our usual pint of ale at this lunch, but by the time we settled in near that fire and dried off a bit, a pint of Tinners Ale started sounding pretty good to Philip and me. Mark ordered his usual cider and Claire a glass of white wine. Life is short, we said to each other, let's have a toast! We toasted the wind and the sea, the dogs and the log fire, and Claire's lovely and stylish backpack headwear, which we decided might become a new fashion trend. We made our menu selections over a plate of hummus and pita with a shared order of crispy salt and pepper squid which the chef served with tangy lime and coriander mayonnaise. If the winds of the Cape hadn't fired our appetites, these small bites certainly did.

For her lunch, Claire chose the fresh local crab sandwich on granary bread which she shared with Mark. It was truly large enough for two. Philip was in the mood for a traditional lunch after all the wind and rain, so he went with the home-cooked ham and free-range duck egg which was served with hand-cut chips. Nearly everything is local here. The fish comes in from Newlyn just seven miles down the coast, and their meat is also local. Most of the vegetables and eggs come from local farms. If you're going to travel halfway around the world for lunch, this is the place to have it. I was ready for chicken, so I chose a dish I've had here before, the chicken stew. I honestly don't know when I've enjoyed lunch this much.

We lingered after our last bites by the fire, chatting and meeting local folks. Claire and Philip wanted to treat Mark and me to lunch on that day, so Claire took the check to the bar to pay where, of course, she engaged the local gentlemen who had stopped in for a pint. I overheard part of their conversation. It started out well enough, exchanging notes about their home in Minneapolis and the fishing industry in the area. But then one of them asked Claire how she liked the ale in the pubs.

"I think it's rather bitter," she said in her usual frank way.

I saw the guy wince a little, but Claire didn't see that. "Bitter?"

"Uh-huh. It tastes like the bottom of the barrel."
He turned to his friend and said, "She doesn't like the ale." Then to Claire, "Have you tried Tribute?" She wasn't sure what Tribute was, I could tell, and she said: "Well, no."

"Proper Job?" he asked. "Doombar? Have you ever had a Betty?" He was raising his voice ever so slightly. Still polite, but a tiny bit of a huff.

"No, not really." Claire was looking for a way to back out of this, but she couldn't help herself, so she asked, "What on earth is a Betty?"

"See?" the fellow said, turning back to his friend, "she's never tried a Betty, and yet she's an authority on our ale. She doesn't even know about Betty." He was referring to Betty Stogs, a beloved local ale brewed in Truro at Skinners. It has won awards and was recently declared the best bitter ale in all of England. "Betty Stogs was reputedly full-bodied, golden-hearted, and just a little fruity," the brewery likes to say, "so we named our beer after her." It's actually quite light and easy to drink. I was debating whether I should try to rescue her, but Philip beat me to it.

He stepped up and took Claire by the elbow, just to allow him to get into this conversation. "Hi Honey," he said. "Did you pay yet?"

She nodded. "We've been discussing the local ale," she said dryly to Philip. And then they backed away a step or two and turned toward the door. I nodded smilingly toward the guy at the bar and then followed them outside. On the way to the car, Claire said, "Well, that was something, wasn't it? They sure love their beer." I bit my tongue.

Before we left the village, we popped into the parish church. The history there told us that this site has had a church on it since the 6th century, or maybe even earlier. The current building isn't that old, or at least parts of it are newer, probably dating from the 13th or 15th centuries. Legend has it that Saint Senara founded this church and village after returning from Ireland with her son, who was by then a bishop.

The whole church was decked out for Christmas. Every local parish club puts up a tree following the annual theme, so the nave was crowded with them. On the church's outside wall, next to the west entry, is a memorial to a fellow called John Davy who was apparently the last person to speak Cornish fluently. It's dated from 1891. The graveyard is said to date from the Bronze Age. There is a legend here that a local cow once ate the bell-rope which had been made of straw, but unless it was a tall critter, it couldn't have gotten very far up the rope.

We lingered for a while, considering all these things. By now it was 2 PM and, holy cow, we had planned that night to be in Truro for Lessons and Carols by 6 PM. Between the wild winds of Cape Cornwall and the long sit by the fire in the Tinners Arms, we had almost forgotten that we were here on our Christmas holidays. We were all ready to get back to our fisherman's cottage, rest a little, do something with our wind-blown hair, dry out our gear, and get prepared for the evening. Off we went.

Chapter 11
Truro Cathedral and a Remarkable Voice

Upstairs in our little cottage, we had two comfortable bedrooms sharing one large bath, so we had to take turns with the shower. We had set it up on a first-come, first-served basis but the hot water was "on-demand" so there would always be enough. Still, it was a bustle to get everyone ready and out the door by four-thirty or five-o-clock. The doors of the cathedral would open at six and seating was limited to the first thousand who showed up. I know, I know, in a small rural town in central Cornwall, wouldn't that seem to be enough? But no. The ushers sometimes have to turn some people away, and, besides, we wanted to get in early to score seats in the choir stalls if we could.

Mark and Philip had been kibitzing together in the back seat since we left Zennor earlier. They were making lists and checking them twice, and I knew they were up to something, probably something pretty delicious for our late supper. Both of these guys could cook. What luck for Claire and me! So, as I came downstairs from my shower, I found them hustling in the door carrying bags and bundles from the local greengrocer, the fish market, and the butcher shop. "What's up, guys?" I asked.

"Oh, nothing. Just a bite for later on..." They tucked it all away and headed up to get ready. Tempted as I was to sneak a peek into their plans, my conscience kept me from it. 'Twas the night before Christmas Eve, after all, and it seemed out of bounds to go around prying into people's secrets. Philip already had something brewing in a slow cooker, but I didn't even lift the lid to peek, just in case Santa was watching.

When everyone was finally nearly ready, I set off on foot to fetch the car. I headed down the Digey toward the sea and at Bumbles Tea Room took a sharp right up Back Road past the St Ives School of Painting and the Penwith Gallery. From there, I hiked onward past the Mermaid, a great spot to dine on local fish and seafood in a room full of church pews, checkered tablecloths, and fishnets. Back Road ends near Smeaton's Pier on Wheal Dream where I turned left and hoofed my way onto the coastal footpath down along the seawall past a tiny beach tucked in among the rocks, Bamaluz Beach. This led me into the Porthmeor parking lot next door to yet another small, local beach, the Porthgwidden.

Parking in St Ives, as in many small fishing villages here, is very limited. We rent a space with our cottage and never park anywhere else. During the busy summer months, most people park out of town and arrive by train or bus. In any case, I hopped into the car and wound my way back toward our cottage just in time to meet my mates who piled in and off we went. To get out of town in the direction of Truro is a dizzying labyrinth leading away from our cottage, down to the sea, a sharp left around the Tate, and another left to drive up the steep Porthmeor Hill. Then there's a jog to the right (or is it to the left?). Down that hill into a traffic circle, taking the second exit from it. From that point, one must drive around a housing development, along what's called the North Terrace, and then merge blindly onto the main road—we hope. We often get lost. Tonight, we were lucky, and soon we were driving back up the peninsula toward Bodmin Moor on the A30.

Claire and Philip were in a merry mood, jabbering about this and that, remembering old Christmas traditions, and finally breaking into a back-seat rendition of *Have Yourself a Merry Little Christmas*, which, of course, Judy Garland had sung in *Meet Me in St Louis*. They didn't remember the words quite correctly, so Mark joined in to help, which created a third version of the song, all being sung at the same time. If the passengers in other cars along the A30 could have heard us, I think they may have called the police. We were quite the little holiday crew, sailing along in the dusk of December.

At the Three Burrows roundabout, we turned onto the A390 and joined some reasonably heavy traffic down into Truro. Truro is the largest "city" in Cornwall, the center of local trade and government, and the site of the only cathedral in the county. This cathedral belongs to the Church of England, of course, and, when it was built starting in 1880, it was the first new cathedral to break ground in England for more than 650 years—ever since they began the work on Salisbury Cathedral in 1220.

This cathedral has three massive towers which are visible from all over town. The architect on the project was John Loughborough Pearson who was heavily influenced by the then-popular Gothic movement, reflecting the early English style. The spires tell it all: the central tower and spire are two-hundred-fifty feet tall, but the western towers are also high, reaching two-hundred feet. We used the towers and signage to navigate our way into the center of town where we parked and found our way into Boscawen Street. Holiday shoppers, carolers, and street vendors filled the streets. It was quite a busy flurry. We all had a little shopping to do so, even though we were nearly at six-o-clock, we wandered off on our own for a while, picking up this or that gift for each other. The shops in central Truro were full of folks just like us, picking up a last-minute item or a few bits of décor for the holiday.

As the cathedral bells began to ring out the six-o-clock hour, though, Mark and I made our way over to the plaza in front of the big church where we met Philip and Claire. People were streaming in from every corner of the square, so we followed the madding crowd. As early as it was, the church was half-filled. We thought maybe we should ask permission to sit in the choir stalls, but no one seemed to be watching very closely, so we just walked forward down the center aisle in a brave little impromptu procession of four. At the front, we marched up the stairs and into the choir stalls where we found some seats that were not marked for the choristers or anyone else and sat ourselves down in them. 'Well,' I thought to myself. 'That was easy. Sometimes the best approach is to just march in, I guess.'

The crazy loud busyness of the streets we had just left now gave way to the near-silence of this space, half-dark, with a low buzz as people whispered to one another *sotto voce*. We met the people seated near us, but in typical English fashion, a somewhat stiff formality was in force. I recall a friend of mine who told me about his move to London. He had asked a British colleague for some advice on how to meet the English people. "Well," his colleague said, "don't ask any personal questions." But when pushed for a bit more advice from his friend, he followed that up with this: "And don't forget that in England, *every* question is a personal question." I took that to heart in the cathedral and kept it safe with the people seated around me.

We had rushed just a little to get to Truro and be on time. Now I could feel the tension of that mad dash leave me as the acolytes and ushers glided about, lighting candles or seating people. Then suddenly the lights were dimmed even further, almost dark. Silence now. A pregnant moment of pure silence in a church filled with a thousand souls.

And then occurred a moment so sublime that I cannot adequately describe it. A single, clear voice, that of a young male chorister, rose up above the dark cathedral, candlelit and otherwise silent. The words of this soloist echoed off the walls and reredos as the choir began to process into its place.

> Once in royal David's city
> Stood a lowly cattle shed,

Where a mother laid her baby
In a manger for his bed:
Mary was that mother mild,
Jesus Christ, her little child.

In 1878 the Royal Cornwall Gazette had reported that the choir of Truro Cathedral would sing a service of carols at ten-o-clock on Christmas Eve. That evening in 1878 was the first-ever service of Nine Lessons and Carols, later made more famous by King's College in Cambridge. It was born here, though, created by the then-bishop of Truro, Edward White Benson, and it's been sung here every Christmas since. The lessons and carols told the story of the birth of Jesus some two-thousand years ago. We're not talking here about carols like *Frosty the Snowman* or *Jingle Bells*. These were *religious* hymns.

So, there we were, a group of friends whom I would say had pretty divergent views about all things religious, and we were sitting in a very sacred ceremony. Philip was raised in a congregational church, one in which ritual and liturgy had very little place. He practiced what he called "secular faith," believing in the common good and in a supreme being, but one who never got directly involved with us humans. Philip felt quite strongly that it's up to us to figure out how to share the planet and live together, and that God—whoever he or she may be—keeps his distance from all our mundane arguments.

Claire, as we have seen, thought that she might become a nun one day, an idea that mainly occurred to Catholic girls in parochial schools, which is precisely Claire's experience. Claire had confessed to me a year ago that she often stopped in a local parish church to "make a visit" but that they rarely show up there on Sunday mornings. "Still," she told me, "I just can't leave it behind. I'd love to find a way back in." They did have a Catholic wedding, and she made me promise that I'd help Philip organize a Catholic funeral if she got hit by a big bus some day. Sitting there in the choir stalls getting ready for Lessons and Carols was something Claire relished, and Philip knew how much this meant to her.

Mark and I were the ones most connected to things churchy; we belonged to a parish and were pretty regular about being at church on the weekends. Mark was raised in a congregational church but really never participated in it. He couldn't embrace all the elements of religion, but we both liked the "time out" each week; we liked being there together, and we also liked the community. For my part, I had long ago shifted my focus from liturgical details and biblical literalism to a practical care-for-the-poor and a build-a-safe-world-for-all understanding. I truly embraced that old "whatever you do for the least of my sisters or brothers, you do for me…" business. Liturgy supported that, but the key was to get busy and make this a better world for everyone, poor and rich alike.

The trappings of liturgy, however, were all around us on this night and the story they were telling sounded like a pretty literal account of Jesus' birth in a manger with shepherds and angels and yadda, yadda, yadda. If prompted, I could have given my old "don't take this story literally" speech, but no one asked.

Fortunately, we were able to overlook the literalism in the storytelling so that being there in the cathedral that night with all its history and warmth was splendid for us all. The various lessons from Scripture and the familiar carols conspired to enchant and move us. As the service came to an end, we were left nearly speechless, which is saying a lot for our crowd. But who could comment? What could we say in addition to what the choir and that remarkable soloist had just sung?

We moved quietly out of the cathedral, jostling with the crowd, and walked slowly to our car. I noticed that Claire had Philip's arm as they strolled in the evening light. Mark slipped his hand into mine as we moved along the quiet, rain-washed street. Christmas lights twinkled on every lamp post. Silent night; holy night.

Chapter 12
Christmas Windows & Home Cooking

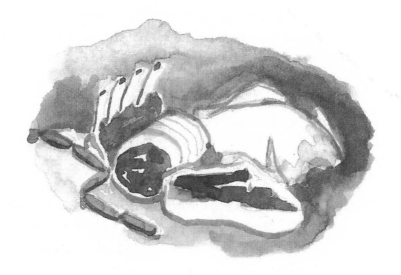

Of course, the sublime silence was shattered almost immediately when I made a left turn instead of a right one leaving the parking lot. A cacophony of voices was now helping me find my way back toward the A390, and I must say, they were all a lot of help. We chattered like seagulls all the way home, energized by the lovely service we had just witnessed and eagerly looking forward to a light supper at the cottage. We had agreed before departing on this journey that we'd have three small plates as our supper for this evening, one from Mark, one from Philip, and one that would apparently appear miraculously from Claire who had made no obvious preparations so far. My job would be to tend the bar. We were excited to get this food liturgy underway!

We parked out at Porthmeor Beach again, and walked together back through the village, alight with holiday cheer and people bustling with Christmas preparations. We could see through the windows that the residents had lighted their trees and candles. Families and friends were gathering. As if in a shadow play, we could see through the translucent window shade in one house a family serving dinner to each other at the table. Had they paused while we watched to give thanks? Or did we all imagine that? We looked away as though we had pried into their private lives. Then we tightened our scarves against the chill and hurried along just a bit more to make our way home.

A little bit of sleet came just as we rounded the corner onto the Digey, just enough to remind us that it is winter even here. We hustled in the door, shook off our coats and scarves, and piled into the cozy living room.

If someone had been looking into our windows just then they would have seen a busy household. One of us lit the fireplace while another lit a batch of fresh candles. Claire got the music playing while I started mixing the drinks. Mark was in the kitchen in a flash, preparing our first course. This would be small plate number one, Philip was number two, and as I mentioned, number three remained a mystery. Dinner in tapas-style. But our preprandial would be in the living room in front of the fire with a cocktail and a first bite.

The cocktail, we had all agreed, should be something quintessentially British, but not ale. We decided on the Sidecar. This drink was created sometime just after World War I in London's Buck's Club at 18 Clifford Street. The recipe says that you start with ice, which seemed very unBritish to us, but then you add an ounce or two (two!) of cognac per person into a cocktail shaker. You add about half that much Grand Marnier and about one third that much fresh lemon juice. The instructions are pretty simple: "Shake well." it says. I can do that. Some mixologists think it's necessary to strain or even double strain this as it's poured, but I like the bits of lemon in the glass. Voila! A Sidecar. Or more accurately, four Sidecars!

The appetizer consisted of local, freshly-smoked salmon served in the English style: on rye toast nestled in cream cheese and capers with a sprinkle of dill. Served with steamed, chilled, and quartered new potatoes with a dollop of garlic aioli, cornichons, and slices of peppered cucumber. Philip served this to us, but he was clear that this was not to be considered one of the three small plates, just in case Claire was planning to cheat. She stuck out her tongue at him, but then they kissed and made up very quickly.

Lessons and Carols already seemed to drift out of our memories now into our recent—but still glowing—past. With the drinks poured, the fire lit, and the salmon platter already half-eaten, we had our first toast to Christmas. Toasting for us was a form of table prayer. In a way, it was more real than the usual memorized prayers because toasts always came from our hearts. We offered them frequently, even in the middle of a meal. We toasted the people present or ones who were absent; the events of the world;

the saints and sinners who had settled this place; the cooks and farmers and shopkeepers; the things that mattered in our lives; and the poor. We had a system for keeping the poor in mind at our table: whenever we indulged ourselves with an excellent meal or an extra luxury, we set aside an equivalent gift of money for people in need. We love our food and wine, but once we take the poor and needy out of the equation, the joy goes out with it. It's only a grand celebration if we carry everyone along.

"To finding ourselves here," Claire started.

"To finding *you* here, my dear," Philip added.

"To finding *us* here," she corrected. "Not to mention finding the damn corkscrew. I think I might have put it in the refrigerator now," she finished.

"To our families," Mark added, "and to that young soloist tonight at the cathedral. Remarkable."

"To us, Honey," I said to Mark, "and to you, Claire and Philip, and to Moley and Ratty, God bless 'em."

"Here! Here!"

"Shouldn't we toast Cape Cornwall? It's hard to believe that we visited there earlier today, but it was just this morning." Cheers went up all around the circle.

Mark was back in the kitchen now putting the final touch on our first small plate. The dining table in our cottage was located adjacent to the kitchen so that one of us could be cooking but not be away from the others, and we all moved out there now. Mark had gotten a bottle of Santi Nello, a Prosecco from Veneto, Italy. So, with the lights low and the candles lit, he served our first plate, a signature dish of his, *Coquilles St Jacques*. He served it on large scallop shells that *he had brought with him* for this evening. (Who does that? That's not all he brought for the kitchen; just hang on.) The dish looked spectacular; he had dusted it with crumbs and browned it perfectly under the broiler. It's a French dish, but he nodded to Cornwall by using succulent Cornish scallops which are known to be among the most excellent seafood in all of England. They come from the fresh, clear water around the Cornish coastline, and the taste and quality are second to none. That and a warm baguette to soak up the sauce was all we needed.

Claire took one forkful of the *Coquilles*, put down her fork, and said, "Oh gosh, Mark. This scallop is so good. How did you do this? It's the best taste of the trip so far. Mmmm..." We all agreed.

Mark served only two scallops per person, just enough for a small plate. He started by making his sauce: a half stick or so of butter (what's not to like?) with a little olive oil added to it. He diced a medium-sized shallot, a single clove of garlic, and a few scallions and sautéed them in the butter, finishing it with white wine, maybe one-third cup. He let the wine cook down just a little. "Use the good wine," he said. "If you don't want to drink a wine you shouldn't cook with it."

Then he made a light roux: flour cooked in a little more butter, and added that with some clotted cream, a very English touch, and as much stock as needed, which isn't very much. He added a bit of

119

lemon juice and a small amount of grated Gruyere, plus a couple spoonsful of chopped parsley. Into this sauce, then, he plunked the scallops, sliced in half the long way, to cook them until lightly done. He had nestled the scallop shells onto a baking sheet with some foil to keep them level during the finishing. Then he scooped this sauce while still hot into those shells, making sure the scallops were evenly distributed, topped them with bread crumbs, a scrape or two of fresh nutmeg (and yes, he brought that with him!) and popped them into the oven to brown and finish. From the oven, they came directly to the table, and that's what he presented to us.

A momentary silence fell upon us all, not so much one of reverence as of delight. We savored each bite of scallop, coated with bits of the shallot and scallions, and the thick sauce filled with flavor, accompanied by that wonderful Prosecco. We used the bread to soak up and wipe off every last drop; it was that good.

As I mentioned, we were making three small plates our supper for the evening. We'd tasted only one so far, and Philip was up next. First, though, a short break was in order. While Philip did his magic on small plate number two and let it rest a few minutes, we polished off the Prosecco and read a few pages from *The Wind in the Willows*. We had left Moley and Ratty, as you recall, sitting by the fire in Ratty's riverside home, telling stories about life on the river.

On their way down the river on that first day, the Mole was curious about a woodland that he could see spreading out in a broad swath to their left and to their right. It was framed by vast meadows and fence lines. It appeared dark and gave Mole a sense of foreboding. And yet, he felt somehow drawn to it in the way one might be attracted to something mysterious like that. To him, this vast forest seemed tremendous, a word that comes from the Latin *temere* meaning, tremble. Indeed, as fascinated as he was by it, drawn toward it, he was also frightened of it. It both made him tremble and at the same time, drew him in.

He asked the Rat about this forest, and Mole could see that his question startled Ratty. The Rat tried to be dismissive; he waved his paw in that direction and told the Mole in no uncertain terms that the Wild Wood was not a place for river-bankers. As strange and exotic as it seemed, Ratty cautioned his friend that he should never go there. Stoats, weasels, rabbits, and squirrels lived there— a mixed lot of characters as far as the Rat was concerned. It may draw you in, he told the Mole, but you could also get lost or hurt— or something even worse. Badger's house was smack in the middle of the Wood, he told the Mole, but otherwise, the Wild Wood was a place for trouble.

Philip was reading at this point. He put down the book and just sat quietly for a minute. "Who hasn't been lured into something attractive? You know, a relationship or a job or, I don't know, some kind of deal that's too good to be true? You know you shouldn't go there, but somehow, you can't seem to help yourself. Lead us not into temptation," he said. Philip was talking about his last job. He was the manager and *maître d'hôtel* of a posh St Paul eatery, but the owner also convinced him to invest money in the restaurant. Philip was hesitant, and I remembered us talking this over several times back then. The owner was something of a schmuck and had made a lot of bad deals with a lot of people. The restaurant business is tough, and Philip knew that, but he thought he was smart enough to navigate the terrain. He got burned when the restaurant closed up one Thursday without warning. Philip lost his job and their money. He always said, though, that he considered that investment to be tuition. He learned a great deal from the whole experience. It was his Wild Wood.

We paused a few minutes in the reading while Philip told us his story again. Our stories, like the one you're reading, form and shape us. Claire poured another round of drinks, and, as he wound up, Philip reminded us that we were in the middle of our supper. We'd almost forgotten. He jumped up to check his dish—everything was just fine and 'on hold.' The beautiful thing about stories like these, we all agreed, is what it awakens within us. In Philip, it stirred memories of lessons learned, but each of us had our own Wild Wood to tell about. Stories have power, as Flannery O'Connor reminded us. "A story is a way to say something that can't be said any other way," she wrote. And for Philip and all of us on this eve of Christmas eve, stories were in the air.

We segued back to the book where, in the meantime, the Mole dropped the whole subject with Ratty. Moley knew that animal etiquette required that he not raise the question again. Animals don't like to discuss matters that may lead to trouble, things such as traps, hunters, and schmucks.

Mole dropped the subject, but not the idea of exploring the Wild Wood one day. For months he bided his time but then one afternoon in early winter while the Rat was busy alternately scribbling poetry and napping, the Mole crept out of the house and made his way into the Wood. As he sauntered along, everything seemed to be just fine. He met the rabbits: pretty nutty bunch, racing around the way they did, but they seemed harmless. He was just beginning to congratulate himself on being brave and wise when he started hearing strange sounds. Soon he was meeting even more unusual creatures. As winter's early dusk began to creep in, and the darkness of the Wood surrounded him, he became frightened. Soon he lost his way. And then the snow started, lightly at first, but soon it became a heavy and deep snowfall. Moley was paralyzed by it all and could not go on.

"Oh my," Philip said, passing the book to Mark. "I've been there."

Finally, lost and alone, Moley tucked himself into the hollow of a tree, covering himself in leaves: shivering, hungry, and wishing he'd never gone there.

But back at the Riverbank, good old Ratty had awakened from his winter nap and realized that the Mole was gone. He could see by following his tracks that Mole had gone into the Wild Wood. Rat knew immediately that he had to follow him so he "strapped a belt round his waist, shoved a brace of pistols into it, took up a stout cudgel that stood in a corner of the hall, and set off for the Wild Wood at a smart pace."

"What a dear friend," Claire said. "I like that Rat."

Soon the Rat, consulting the rabbits and other forest creatures, found poor Moley holed up and afraid in his tree refuge. Together, they began the journey back to the Riverbank, but it was late and dark and snowy. Eventually, as they plowed through the deep snow, they stumbled accidentally on a metal door scraper, way out there in the middle of what seemed to be nowhere. In fact, the poor Mole cut his leg quite badly on it. To Mole, a door scraper in a remote part of the Wild Wood meant very little, but to the clever Rat, it was much more significant. He knew they had stumbled onto something big. "But don't you see what it MEANS, you—you dull-witted animal?" cried the Rat impatiently.

At the Rat's insistence, they both began to scrape and dig and paw their way through the snow near the door scraper until a doormat came into view. "What did I tell you?" cried the Rat in great triumph. But poor Mole was still in the dark. He was confused as to why an old doormat should mean *anything* during this crisis. But again, the Rat took charge, and they continued digging and scraping and scratching until at last the Rat's cudgel struck something that sounded hollow. Pulling the snow away from it, they could see that they had found a door. And, on the door, a small, brass plate, neatly engraved with the name: BADGER.

And at this exciting point, we had to leave the story. We were all charmed by Moley and Ratty, and found ourselves identifying, first with one and then the other. "I can't believe we've only been here for a couple of days," Mark said before we left the living room. "These stories fill up the time and make it disappear, don't they?" We agreed that having the leisure to sit around reading and chatting and was a real luxury, a real gift that we were giving to each other.

But at this point, Philip, dressed in an apron and carrying a wooden spoon, appeared in the doorway of the kitchen to announce that he was ready and it was time for small plate number two. We all grabbed our wine glasses and headed for the table. Whatever it was Philip was about to serve us, we had smelled it in the cottage since before we left for St Just and Cape Cornwall that morning. We all saw him put something into a crockpot while we were having breakfast, but he didn't say much about it. Now he opened a stunning bottle of red wine from Saint-Émilion and poured a glass for each of us. Then he brought his dish to the table on four small plates and presented it to us. It looked like nothing more than a quesadilla. We all stared at our plates.

"Mexican?" someone asked.

"Fusion," he told us. "Just taste it first."

I sank my fork into the quesadilla—which Philip had browned perfectly—and took my first bite of it. Wow! It was delicious! Tender, full of flavor. A complete change from the scallops of the last course. Claire was next: "How did you do this, Honey?" she asked. "I was with you all day. When did you have time…?" He waved his hand as if to say, 'But I'm a chef, and I've got my secrets.'

By now we had deciphered his dish. It was a beef brisket quesadilla. Instead of refried beans as a base, he used mashed potatoes with horseradish on which he sprinkled diced parsley. The mash and brisket were full of flavor! And the dry Bordeaux he served with it highlighted both the wine and the dish. It was perfect. Mark wanted to know how he prepared this.

I started with Bill, he told us, you know, the butcher on duty at the shop in Tregenna Place. Mark and I knew immediately that he had gotten good advice; we've been taking Bill's suggestions for many years. Harvey Brothers Butchers is a great shop. They have their own farm, located just a few miles west of St Ives on the coast between Pendeen and St Just. It's a beautiful location overlooking the Celtic Sea, and this is where they breed and raise their cattle. The critters roam freely and graze naturally on grass. They have less stress than anyone I know! The result is obvious: it is very high-quality Cornish beef. I'd say this farm is less than nine miles from our cottage, which is a very low number of "food miles," indeed.

Bill had trimmed the brisket for Philip last evening while we were all out around town doing a little Christmas shopping. Philip needed only a small, two-pound piece and Bill accommodated him. Philip then salted the brisket according to Bill's suggestion, wrapped it in plastic wrap, and tucked it into the back of the frig. This morning he dug out an old slow cooker from the cupboard of the cottage—he had spotted in there on that first night—and heated it up. He was also hoping to find a blender for his sauce, but alas, there was none there. He mixed up a bit of mustard with some brown sugar and a couple of seasonings he had brought with him. (Both Philip and Mark travel with seasonings and spices, causing Claire and me to simply roll our eyes and order out.)

He rubbed the brisket with this mustard mixture this morning and popped it into the slow cooker. Bill had sent him home with a couple of strips of locally cured bacon, at no charge of course and on the principle that you can't cook a decent brisket without it. In any case, Philip had obediently used the bacon to brown up some onions which he added to the cooker before adding a bay leaf, a bottle of Cornish ale, and a couple of cups of beef stock.

Then he went with us to Cape Cornwall, the Tinners Arms, and Truro for Lessons and Carols. When we got home that evening, he checked his cooker and was delighted to find a very tender and savory brisket. He cooked his potatoes until soft but not mushy and created a "dry mash" with that touch of horseradish. He spread the mash on the quesadilla, added a generous amount of very thinly sliced brisket and some of the onions, and added the top crust. Then he carefully browned each one in a sauté pan and added a sprinkle of cheddar cheese just before coming to the table.

Of course, after our first bite of this, there had to be some toasts. Claire began. "To my renaissance man of a husband," she said. "I'm glad you found your way out of the Wild Wood."

"I couldn't have done it without your love, darling."

Yeah, Philip, here's to you and this quesadilla. It's pretty darn good."

"To all of us," Philip said. "It's so great that we're still friends even though we know each other's stories." Cheers went up all around the table. We cleaned our plates, including a bit of leftover brisket, and finished off the Bordeaux.

But a question did linger in the air. What about small plate number three? These first small plates had been lovely and satisfying—scallops and brisket—but they were truly tapas-sized. It was getting late now, nearly ten-thirty—we hadn't gotten back from Truro until almost nine-o-clock—and we were all feeling a little sleepy. Yet, there was one more course to go: that mysterious third plate.

While we were all chattering about our plans for tomorrow, Claire announced a brief break while she tended to her culinary contribution. We all pitched in to clean up the kitchen and load the dishwasher while she left the room and, as it turns out, left the cottage. She dashed down the Digey to Fore Street, took a quick left, and ran up the stairs to a small joint behind the car park at the Sloop Inn. The three of us didn't even know she had left the house and were in the dark about what was next, but that didn't stop us from opening another bottle of wine, this one a very crisp white: a delicious Pinot Grigio from Trentino in Italy.

Within minutes, Claire was back, carrying a large bundle of very hot fish and chips from the Balancing Eel, the shop around the corner. How she spotted the best fish n' chips in town and arranged with them to have her order ready at precisely ten-thirty was indeed miraculous. We put down another round of small plates on the table, topped off our wine glasses, and heartily dived into this delicious and final small plate. You'd have thought none of us had eaten a morsel in the past week. We cleaned up every crumb of fish and every last chip, wiping the grease off our mouths as we went. It was perfect, and Claire got excellent marks for her contribution. Philip was the one this time who said to Claire, "I must know how you made this, Sweetie."

"Well, Honey," she purred, exaggerating the *Honey*, "I started early this morning on a fishing boat off Smeaton's Pier..." She was mocking our two chefs but only a little. Laughter all around! In truth, Claire's dish was a perfect finish to our December 23rd English buffet.

The eve of Christmas Eve was drawing to a close for all of us. Fat and happy, we trundled off to bed with, dare I say it, visions of sugar plums... Well, at least we had memories of scallops, brisket, and fried fish dancing in our heads. And we could all still hear the strange and beautiful silence of the cathedral, pierced by that stunning solo voice, calling us all to Christmas.

Chapter 13

Mrs. Poole and Tea for Two

Mark and I had brought with us from home four sturdy Christmas stockings each with a name on it: Claire, Philip, Mark, Bill. Early on Christmas Eve morning, we hung these by the chimney with care and hoped that St Nick might do the rest. Sure enough, throughout the day on the 24th, small gifts and stocking stuffers found their way into the cottage so that, by early evening, it looked just a little like our commitment to a non-commercial Christmas had waned.

St Ives is free of big box stores and car trunks full of gifts. Local folks usually can be seen hurrying along the lane with one or two small gifts, so few that the wrapping paper doesn't need to come in jumbo packs. The local custom is to keep Christmas with a laid-back, intimate, and personal gift.

But there was some shopping to get done nonetheless. So out we all went, in singles or pairs, to pick up a little gift here or there. It's a tricky way to give gifts at Christmas: we spend less money and buy fewer items, but the planning and choosing are much more difficult. It's easy to throw a dozen gifts under the tree and hope that one or two might be right. To put just one or two there is a more significant risk. I've always said that, as a writer, it's much more difficult for me to write a 400-word essay about something than it is to write down every thought I ever had about that subject.

We were all on foot today; the car stayed in its car park for the entire day. Mark and I started our day in a coffee shop on Fore Street with "white coffee" and a sausage roll. White coffee, of course, is how the Brits—and us when we're trying to sound like locals—order their coffee with milk. *Café au lait* in French. *Café con leche* in Spanish. And sausage rolls speak for themselves: they're the same in every language. We carried our last cup of coffee with us and headed down Fore Street toward Trewyn Gardens. This garden is on Bedford Road near Richmond Place, only a few steps from the center of town but there are never many visitors.

As we rounded the corner from Fore Street onto Lifeboat Hill, right where Madeleine's Tea Room used to be—now called Market Place Tea Room, named after the building across the street—Mark saw two women bustling along Lifeboat Hill, both in long overcoats. But, as he watched, a fat, unseen seagull that had perched on the edge of the roof above them made a rather large deposit—plop!—on the back of one woman's coat! She and her friend shrieked, quickly cleaned it off, and hurried along. But Mark was so amused he had to stop and laugh. I hadn't seen any of this because I had paused momentarily and was window shopping at the St Ives Bookseller, which is very near. At this point, because the universe always makes sure that it's in balance, and just as I came around the corner, the first gull's cousin (they're all cousins, I think) followed suit with a discharge of its own, and it landed—plop! plop!—directly on Mark's hat! 'Don't you dare laugh,' I said to myself. But one glance from Mark with an 'oh poop' look in his eye, and I thought I was going to wet my pants laughing—being careful to move away from beneath the seagulls, of course. We cleaned him up, got a second cup of coffee, and headed to Trewyn Garden.

To this day, all I need to say to him is, "Remember that seagull in St Ives?"

In the park, we sat for a spell on one of the benches within view of the whole place, drinking our coffee and repeating the seagull story over and over again, laughing until we were exhausted from it. Gratefully, we were the only visitors in the garden that morning because we were entirely out of control. Finally, after fifteen minutes of this, we settled down and started to look around the garden in which we were sitting.

Trewyn is an almost-forgotten garden, one that is very peaceful, well-maintained, and full of blooming subtropical plants at any time of year. There's a memorial to Barbara Hepworth here called *Megalith* by John Milne. Barbara Hepworth's studio was called Trewyn, and it is quite close. She died in a fire there in 1975. John Milne was her pupil, assistant, and close friend; he made this sculpture in memory of her. A megalith, of course, is a large stone that's usually part of a monument of some kind; I think Milne saw Hepworth herself as such a megalith.

We were just up the street from her *Madonna and Child* in the Lady Chapel of the parish church; carved in honor of her son, Paul. This memorial to her death stands almost within view of the monument to her son's death. This is how life and death turn around each other, we said. Mother memorializes son. Soon the mother is memorialized as well. This peaceful garden seemed the right place to wish her a Happy Christmas.

Afterward, we hiked up Chapel Street toward the North Terrace where we crawled through several antique and second-hand shops. Charity shops are popular throughout England. They're organized to contribute their profits to the heart fund, a children's welfare group, or some other good cause, and they're a great place to find bargains. At this time of year, they're well stocked and busy. Mark loves these shops, and he can linger quite a while in them, so I left him there momentarily— we needed a little privacy to shop for each other, after all.

Around the corner, the public library was having a used book sale, which was too good to miss. I found many tables full of used books, each with a library code on it. As I was poking through the books, I put my hand by accident on a copy of *The Wind in the Willows*, of all things. Of course, I had to have it for Claire and

Philip. Books are somewhat bulky and difficult to carry home, but this was a real find. I grabbed it and shopped for a while longer, but I knew that Mark would be looking for me soon, so I headed to the front of the library to pay.

A volunteer was at the front desk, waiting to take my money. She was wearing a name tag that read "Mrs. Poole," and she had blue-tinted hair. Her posture was very erect, and her glasses hung on a chain around her neck. I decided that she was an elementary school teacher. Mrs. Poole took one look at the book, and then she looked up at me, apparently deciding why I might want this particular title. "Your children will love this book," she said.

"I haven't any children."

"Oh, that's too bad. Your children would have loved this. Perhaps you can find some children to give it to." I was about to explain, but she segued quickly into a rather long, rambling complaint about the rain we had that morning and how it had come in from the east, which it rarely does. "Mortimer knows about the weather," she assured me with a knowing, confident nod. "He has a naval background." She seemed very proud of this.

I presumed that Mortimer was the odd-looking fellow in Wellingtons who was standing at a table behind her. He wore wire-rimmed glasses that were slightly too small for his face and a baggy sweater with patches on the sleeves. Naval background or not, I decided he was a pharmacist. Retired. He was sorting books by size back there and packing them in boxes. I told Mrs. Poole that I hadn't noticed the direction from which the rain had come, and thought to myself, 'Why are we talking about the weather? I only wanna buy this book.'

"Nasty stuff, that," Mortimer added, joining our conversation. I think he was referring to the rain. "You have to be ready for it." Which may have explained the Wellies.

It was at this point that Mrs. Poole realized that I was not British, but Canadian. I'm an American, of course, but to her, Canada seemed to suit me best; I think she had Canada on her mind. She and Mortimer had recently traveled to Winnipeg to visit her aging aunt. In the next several moments, I learned a lot more about Mrs. Poole than I had bargained for. All in all, I found it hard to believe that this woman had a living aunt because I judged her to be near eighty herself. I tend to misjudge women's ages, though, and have some sad stories to tell about that sometime.

"I say," Mortimer began, "how's that PM of yours getting along with those Americans?" But Mrs. Poole seemed to be in charge of everything Mortimer discussed and promptly changed the subject.

"I thought the food they served was quite odd," she said. "My niece served us poutine: nothing more than skinny chips, fried cheese curds, and brown gravy. Very odd, indeed. How you people can eat such, such, oh, I don't know, such..."

"I had a pork chop," Mortimer threw in, clearing his throat, and I think this was the beginning of a story, but Mrs. Poole still had the floor, and I suspect she rarely surrendered it to poor Mortimer. I could not believe she was trashing a great Canadian dish like poutine, and I felt, suddenly, very Canada-defensive. If she wants to talk about strange food, I thought I might mention tripe and stargazy pie, but I restrained myself.

"And the way you drive, you Canadians," Mrs. Poole interrupted him. "Honestly. The motorways were positively hideous." Then she paused and looked out the window momentarily.

"Go to the loo, dear," she then said to poor Mortimer. I looked at him; he looked self-consciously down at his boots, and then obediently shuffled off to pee. "I have to remind him," she said. "He forgets that he needs to urinate every two hours," which was far more information than I wanted.

At least we had wandered off the subject of Canada, so I seized the moment to ask, "How much for the book, then?"

"One pound, please."

"One pound? That seems quite inexpensive."

"Well, we're a charity," she said with a sniff. I paid her the pound and then added all the odd coins I had in my pocket and told her to put it in the library kitty."

"Well, aren't you Canadians generous?"

I tucked the book into my knapsack and scooted out the door before Mr. Poole returned from the loo.

I came out of the library and found Mark standing under an awning because a light misty rain had blown in. He was watching the passersby and waiting for me. We turned left and headed down what is called "Street an Pol" where we found a local, farmers' market in the Guildhall. Being gardeners ourselves, we can never pass up a chance to check out someone else's home-grown produce. There were a lot of root vegetables, lots of brussels sprouts and, in one stall, a huge pile of freshly harvested cauliflower.

I had noticed earlier that Mark was admiring two small pottery jars in one of the charity shops in High Street so, when he got into a long conversation with a local farmer in the Guildhall, I hoofed my way back up the street to discreetly buy those for his Christmas stocking. When I rejoined him, they were still talking about winter vegetable raising in Cornwall. While they decided whether the manure should go down in the fall or not (is there any question?), I did some shopping: brussels sprouts which are a traditional Cornish Christmas dish, along with a few freshly dug potatoes, carrots, and onions.

We walked from there back up the hill into Tregenna Place to find Bill, the butcher. Sure enough, he was on duty as always. We were shopping for Christmas dinner, and he had just one last standing rib roast remaining. We grabbed it. "When they're gone, they're gone," he told us. "You got the last one." He and Mark had a long conversation about the best way to cook this precious roast so, again, I did some shopping. I picked up a jar of goose fat to use with the potatoes (more about this goose fat later) and beef stock for the au jus. Bill sent us on our way with a "Happy Christmas, fellas!" Afterward, we picked up some local cold meats and Cornish cheese for tonight's appetizers. Philip and Claire were providing the dessert for Christmas, so all we needed to add was the first course which we decided would be a beet salad on rocket with chèvre and honey.

Even though we were now lugging Christmas dinner around with us, we agreed that it was time for a cup of tea—and we knew the perfect place for it. We walked back toward the parish church, turning right when we got there and landed at #17 St Andrew's Street. It's a small shop called, simply, Coasters Tea Room.

Tea for two with scones. And the scones' purpose was mainly to serve as a vehicle for the home-made jam and clotted cream. This clotted cream was produced right here in the county of Cornwall, but Devon is more famous for their version of it. Interestingly, in Devon, the cream is traditionally spread on a scone first and then topped with the jam. In Cornwall, it's the opposite: jam first, then cream. One must get this right! We're talking here about what is called "double cream." It's a thick cream which is silky and delicious, skimmed from the surface of milk as it rises to the top. The English certainly know their way around a scone. Oh, my.

We took a small table in the window of the tea shop which gave us ringside seats to watch the passersby. The tea room is located at a point on St Andrew's where the Coast Path intersects (for those who want it) with city streets. This being Christmas Eve, people were coming and going in small groups, laughing together, arm-in-arm, tucking a package under this arm or a sheet of wrapping paper under that one. Soon a priest came hurrying past, and he seemed to be murmuring to himself, most likely rehearsing his sermon for that night. Then along came a young man carrying a suitcase: was he coming home for the holidays? We watched a small family arrive by car and unload their entire Christmas celebration, the tree and all, while other vehicles patiently waited on St Andrew's. The people-watching was endlessly fascinating—a river of life passing by our window, just as it had for Moley on his first day along with riverbank—but soon enough we had drunk our tea, so we wrapped ourselves up in our scarves again and headed out.

There's an art gallery just up the street from Tea Room, at the corner of Street an Pol and St Andrew's, just where Skidden Hill joins them. It's the Waterside Gallery. The proprietor, we're pretty sure, is the daughter of a leading St Ives artist, Terry Whybrow, whose work we admire. He was born in 1932 in St Pancras, London. Before he moved to Cornwall, he worked as a furniture designer. He's been in St Ives since 1980 and is a full-time painter, even as he now nears 90 years of age. His works are there at the Waterside but also at the Penwith Gallery on Back Road, closer to our cottage. They're stunning; it's hard to take our eyes off them.

He's been influenced by the abstract movement which had been prominent there since the mid-twentieth century. In particular, two leading figures in that movement were Ben Nicholson and Sir Terry Frost. Nicholson was married to Barbara Hepworth, of course, from 1938 to 1951. Frost studied at the St Ives School of Painting where he mounted his first solo show of mainly abstract works in 1947. But for Whybrow, there would be an eventual reversal of the modernist trend. The abstract shapes and forms which he produced in his early works yielded to his interest in still-lifes—mainly fruit and bowls. It's for these latter works that he is most famous today. When you view his paintings, you find in them a quiet, peaceful, and almost gentle nature. His background as a furniture designer shows through because his images are structurally meticulous.

Terry's beloved wife, Marion, died in 2015. She was a significant force in documenting the arts in St Ives and Cornwall, publishing a large number of books including *St Ives 1883-1993, Portrait of an Art Colony*, easily still the most comprehensive book of its kind. She also wrote novels, supported women in the arts, and was a force in getting the Tate to open in St Ives.

We lingered a while in the Waterside admiring his and other works, but we finally decided not to purchase one today. We tucked it in the back of our minds for another visit. As we stepped outside into St Andrew's Street, a chill overtook us briefly. We bundled up and headed back toward the cottage. On the way, we were still in no hurry, so we ducked into one or two more small shops, picking up this or that for Claire and Philip. As we passed the Cornish Bakery on Fore Street, we couldn't resist so we popped in to share a pasty for lunch. Or maybe it was two pasties and a sausage roll that we shared. In any case, for both of us after such a "strenuous" morning, we were ready to head home.

Chapter 14
Winter Holidays & the Back-Street Bistro

The fisherman's cottage was warm and inviting when we arrived home. Carols were playing, and someone had lit the fire. Philip was upstairs wrapping up a few gifts for St Nick. Claire was out shopping on her own. Mark and I had little gifts to tuck into the stockings and small chore that needed doing. It seemed as though the day, unstructured as it was, moved quickly toward dusk and Christmas Eve. Excitement was in the air, a thrill about all that was to come in the evening.

We were all hoping for a wonderful holiday together, and hope is a strong, driving force for people. It's not so much a feeling or an emotion as it is a state of being, a way of seeing the world and living in it. Hope stands above the harsh realities that sometimes surround us. It's that ray of light we see on the horizon, even amid darkness in our lives or in the world. Is hope foolish? It might be, but then again, every great development began as a foolish idea.

Here in Cornwall, they say their hope is not so much that the sea will one day grow calm; they've lived next to the sea and lost too many family members to its moods to hope in that. Instead, they hope they can learn to navigate the sea, even when it's stormy. They hope they can know when to stay ashore and when to venture out, when to go it alone and when to call for help. It's hope mixed with realism. As an old proverb puts it: pray to God but row away from the rocks. They've taken that seriously here.

The winter holidays—whether Christmas, Hanukah, the Solstice, or the New Year—bring out hope in people. Like the fishermen of old St Ives, we hope we can navigate the sometimes-stormy seas of this time of year. We hope we'll have enough sense to call for help if we need it. And regardless of our situation in life, this season produces hope in our hearts. Can we be generous to each other as a society? Can we care for this old earth? Can we experience the conversion to kindness and charity that Ebenezer Scrooge did? We hope so.

Every year, in fact, brings fresh hope, and every year, like this one, there was a thrill in the air as Christmas Eve approached. We were always eager to get the celebration underway!

And indeed, our evening at the fisherman's cottage got underway for us about five-thirty as the winter darkness settled in. We began with a glass of wine and a small appetizer plate of those local meats and Cornish cheeses. We gathered around the fire and chatted together about the adventures of our day and the ghosts of Christmases past. In the background, Karen Carpenter was singing from that fabulous holiday album of hers.

Our Claire had, in her usual way, met a lot of local people. She darted into the Fore Street Methodist Church as she passed it because there was a lot of commotion there and she hates to miss a party. In fact, there was some sort of Christmas tree festival going on and, meanwhile, some ladies from the church were packing up food boxes for the needy. Claire joined them for that as well as for a cup of tea and a piece of mince pie. Afterward, she walked through town and shopped a bit, but she told us she was deep in her own thoughts, walking without really going anywhere.

"This place," she told us, "there's something about this place. I don't know. Maybe it's the people here, or how the light comes in over the sea. I'm not sure, but ever since St Mawgan and those nuns, my heart feels like it's at the edge of my chest, about to burst out. Do you guys feel it?"

"Every time we visit here," I said. "It's why we keep coming back. We rush our way through the air travel and car trip but as soon as we set foot in this village, we're at home."

"I do think it's the light," Mark said. "The color of the light is so— I don't know—so *tactile* almost. I can see how artists have found a home in this place. I could paint here."

"And yet you never have?" Philip asked.

"Oh, I know, I should probably paint, but I don't want to make the commitment. It means schlepping lots of gear, and it's tough to travel with wet oil on a canvas. It's a pain in the ass. And besides, I'm not the only one here every year; I share it with Bill, and what's he going to do while I paint?"

"You could write something," Claire said, turning to me. "You're always scribbling notes and writing things down. You can write, and Mark can paint, and Philip and I will live here as your servants."

"I like the sound of this. When can you start? But what I want to know, Claire, is: were you so deep in those thoughts of yours that you forgot to do your Christmas shopping?"

"Oh, don't you worry, Billsy, Santa found something for you even though you probably weren't a very good little boy this year." She called me by my most intimate pet name, Billsy. It's reserved only for Mark and very close friends. I liked it.

For his part today, Philip told us, he had discovered the charity shops in town and had spent his morning pouring through used things looking for treasures that he couldn't live without. He also found a few treasures that, as it turned out, the rest of us would carry home because he thought we couldn't live without them either! When he got tired of dusty books, he walked up past the old counting-house in Market Place and up Bedford Road, past the Hotel Queens and onward up that hill nearly to the top. When he finally turned around to head back, he headed down Ayr Street which brought him past the Hepworth Museum and down onto Fore Street.

Like Claire, he was ambling along, window shopping, turning things over in his mind. Before he knew it, he had walked all the way down to the harbor where he heard a crowd of people that sounded like they were having fun. They woke him from his reverie. He followed the noise and eventually landed at the Sloop Inn's outside patio. It was a sunny afternoon with a bit of chill in the air, but the place was crowded. "I hadn't had lunch," he said, "so I poked my head inside—a great buzz, good smells, and beer—what else would I have been looking for?. I had a burger and a pint; it was delicious."

The Sloop Inn is an old pub in St Ives located on the harbor where Philip found it. It's one of the oldest inns in Cornwall and local folks claim that it's been in business since "circa 1312." I think the "circa" is a pretty broad estimate. The present building is newer than that, probably dating from the 17th century which, by our American standards, is still very old. The Sloop has always been a favored haunt of artists including Victorian artist, Louis Grier. His paintings are in museums now, but many of them started life right here, hanging in the Sloop.

At any rate, we poured a bit more wine as we savored this Christmas Eve moment together. We had nearly an hour before our dinner reservations, though, and Mark was already eyeing an item or two in the Christmas stockings. Oh fine, we all agreed. We'd sneak in a little early Christmas gift now. Why not? Who made the rules if not us?

Eager Mark got us rolling by presenting a truly gorgeous set of handmade, block-printed greeting cards depicting Philip and

Claire's front door at their home in Minneapolis. They were touched to their toes. Block printing is time-consuming. The artist has to remove whatever part of the block he *doesn't* want to show when he inks and prints. Therefore, each rendering requires making three or four blocks, one for each color. This was a three-color-plus-black print. Mark has an incredible ability as an artist to show people the beauty that is already around them. He absolutely captured the welcome people feel at that doorway, and for Claire, it was like a welcome mat, ushering her into a new chapter of her life at that house.

Then Claire, not to be outdone, presented Mark and me with a framed photograph of the two of us, standing on the stoop of our front porch at the farm in Pine County, smiling like we were the happiest two guys in the world, and maybe we are. We were in work clothes—there was a lot of hard, physical labor involved with owning that farm for sixteen years—and we were tan and fit. We weren't exactly sure when she shot this, but it really showed how much we enjoyed that farm while we had it. It's a treasured picture to this day.

Good grief, I thought, these have been very clever and personal gifts. I don't suppose any of my funny gifts would be appropriate right now—we each had a couple of odd and strange little gifts for each other—so, I thought this was the time to pull out *the book*. I had inscribed it with a very personal message, and Mark joined me in making it a gift from the two of us. It turned out to be a lovely edition, illustrated by Ernest Shepard and published by Scribner, the book's original publisher. Its library stamp on the spine only added to its charm. When Claire saw it, she squealed with delight. "You're kidding, right?" Philip said. "Where on earth did you ever find this? Oh my, Claire, they've given us our own copy of *Wind in the Willows*. Oh my gosh. I don't know what to say."

It's funny with friends like these. You go along with people, busy with activities, making meals, sharing stories, but then along comes a moment that is somehow more intimate. At those times, you have a choice. You can either lean into the emotions or avoid them. Avoiding them is common: you crack a joke, change the subject, leave the room, or downplay the feeling. But Philip was correct when he said he didn't know what to say. He was truly speechless. In the face of our friendship, there are no words. The gift said what words could not. We leaned into the feelings on this occasion; we all gave each other a warm hug. Lovely. Happy Christmas, indeed.

With that, our wine had run out, and we all agreed that the rest of the gift-giving would wait until after supper; our reservation was now at hand. We had spent our time very well together so far this evening: telling the story of each gift's provenance and offering commentary and general hurrahs as we went. No need to rush through having fun, as Mark often said. We wanted to take our time getting to the restaurant as well, so we left the cottage and headed for St Andrew's Street with plenty of time to get there.

As we walked down Fore Street, we were arm in arm, strolling more than walking. The town was bustling, and we had no hurry tonight—and what a lovely thing that is all by itself. We sauntered along, window shopping and chatting. When we got to the parish church at the end of Fore Street, we slipped by it to the right and onto St Andrew's. We took Claire and Philip up to the Waterside to see in the windows those works by Terry Whybrow that we hadn't bought earlier in the day.

Then we window shopped another small gallery next door: Armstrong & Wing, an antique dealer, next door to the Half Moon Gallery, next door to the Longships Gallery, next door to the St Ives Framing and Gallery, which is next door to a restaurant known then as the Back Street Bistro where we had a reservation for eight-o-clock. This is St Ives; you can't go far without stumbling into a gallery, café, or small shop.

As we entered the Bistro, we immediately found ourselves in a warm room with rustic wooden tables and artwork hanging in every available spot. The art is odd and quirky and, along with the rugs, the stone floors, old lamps, and classic windows, the whole place had a bohemian feel to it. It was alive with the buzz of happy diners and Christmas carols. The bistro team was welcoming and warm. It almost felt like our own dining room.

There's a sign at the entry that apologizes on behalf of everyone: "I'm sorry for what I said when I was hungry," it says, which we're sure cannot be meant for *after* the meal. We'd all been charmed by our intimate chatter as we walked out this evening, by the first glass of wine at home, and now by the warm light and friendly staff of the Bistro. No one needed to apologize for anything on this evening, Christmas Eve.

The chef created his menu from local foods as much as possible, but with an urbane twist, almost French. We decided to share two openers, and the staff at the Bistro divided them for us and presented them beautifully. Claire and Mark wanted to share the Cornish white crab, red chili, and coriander egg rolls. The chef served them with a sweet chili dipping sauce and tiny coriander shoots. Philip and I, meanwhile, shared the char-grilled halloumi-covered flatbread. Halloumi is a semi-hard cheese from Cypress. It melts at a reasonably high point so it can be grilled as it was this evening. Grilling dramatically heightens the flavor. They served the flatbread with marinated peppers and lightly dressed greens.

There was no rush at any point in the evening. We enjoyed the conversation and the food at a slow pace. This slow pace, which we had set on the first day outside the Carmelite monastery in St Mawgan, had become the theme of our week whether we were eating, drinking, reading, or shopping. It felt for each of us that we were learning a new skill: going slow.

Our dinners arrived in due time, and they matched the quality of the starters. There was a classic beef bourguignon made with St Just beef rump, parmesan mash, Chantenay carrots, and a playful puff pastry twist. Chantenay carrots seem to be everywhere these days in the cuisine of England. They're short, stout carrots with light orange flesh and reddish cores. They're sweet!

Another plate was of a slow-roasted St Buryan pork belly. The chef served it with sweet potato fondant, a creative apple crumble, and St Ives black pudding—all swimming in a pretty cider & thyme reduction. It was seriously delicious, and I love a good pork belly. St Buryan is a small town about 5 miles west of Penzance, which certainly qualifies as local. It was perfectly tender.

Mark loves his fish, so he went for the roasted fillet of Cornish hake which was served on a bed of sautéed kale and placed beside a pea pesto, the likes of which I had never tasted before. The whole filet was sitting atop a truffle mash decked out with a citrus butter sauce.

And how well do we know our friend, Philip? We guessed it, and he came through with the coq au vin. The chef served this classic dish beside a gorgeous pile of Lyonnaise potatoes—thinly sliced, fried in butter, dressed in parsley—which paired perfectly with the chicken. The plate included a homemade sausage and lightly dressed greens.

"Merry Christmas to our dear friends," Philip toasted, raising his glass. "Thank you for bringing us to this special place on earth. I can see why you love it here so much."

"And here's to Maggie, one of the women who picked up a food basket this afternoon at the church. I can't get her out of my mind. Three kids at home, no husband, really tough sledding for her. We tucked in a few extras for the kiddies."

"Probably the most important gift you'll give anyone this year," someone added.

"A merry Christmas to us all. God bless us, everyone!"

Well, for goodness sakes. By this time, we were all gaga over this bistro. To top it all off, the waiters came around distributing Christmas crackers, which became quite a sensation as various tables of diners shared in the fun. I must say, it was almost like being in your own dining room at home with long-lost relatives.

It was at this point that we swore a pact to have only two meals tomorrow, Christmas Day. The one saving grace of this evening regarding our waistlines was that we declined the desserts. The truth is that we were all ready to go home. We knew we had Mr. Badger waiting for us there. We had left poor Moley and Ratty at his front door last night, still shivering in the cold. But also, Claire had managed to pick up some locally made shortbread biscuits earlier that day, and we imagined them with a swallow or two of Port which she had also procured. As we said goodnight to the staff at the restaurant and walked down St Andrew's Street toward the parish church and our cottage, we all felt that we had the excellent fortune of dear friends, shared meals, and good humor.

Once home, we settled in around the fire—all of us now in our jammies—the Port standing on the coffee table and cookie crumbs gathering from the shortbread. We shared the few small remaining gifts we had chosen for each other and when the stockings were empty, and the room was a mess of paper, ribbons, and tags, we pulled the book out from under it all and returned to the home of Mr. Badger.

Chapter 15

Mr. Badger

There is no creature on earth onto whose doorway you would like to stumble in a lousy storm more than that of Mr. Badger. Once again, we passed the book around the circle, each of us reading a page or two, and our various voices served to carry us back into the Wild Wood where Mole and Rat were still outside Badger's door where we had left them.

If you recall, the Rat was in charge of their escapade at this point, and he had ordered the Mole to hang onto the bell-rope and ring the doorbell with all his might. Meanwhile, the Rat was pounding on the door with his stout cudgel. Then they waited. It's difficult to be patient when you've got cold feet, but they waited on the doormat, and waited, and waited. Finally, they could hear someone shuffling along the hall in his slippers, and they were relieved. Mr. Badger cracked open the door a few inches only to warn whoever was out there that being disturbed so late on such a night better be worthwhile. But when he heard Rat's voice, Badger changed his tone and cheerfully welcomed the two cold animals into his house. "Come along into the kitchen," he told them. "There's a first-rate fire there, and supper and everything."

And so, the tale unfolded as they warmed themselves, ate well, and told their story to Badger. He had seated them in front of the fire just as we were sitting here tonight in our little cottage. As they came into Badger's kitchen, the Mole and Rat could see all of Badger's clean and shiny plates winking from their shelves. Hanging from the rafters were hams, herbs, and baskets of onions and eggs. It was a friendly kitchen, one in which strangers felt welcome and in which wonderful meals would be served. The brick floor was ruddy and clean, the ceiling smoky from the fireplace, and the old oaken chairs were worn shiny.

Badger had gotten them into cozy dressing gowns and slippers, and he had tended to the injury that Mole suffered when he cut his leg on the boot scraper outside Badger's door. He bathed it with warm water and took care to seal up the cut with sticking-plaster. Mole felt as good as new, if not better.

153

Claire's voice choked a little as she read this last line. She put the book down in her lap and looked at Philip next to her and then at Mark and me. We allowed the comfortable silence to surround us. "I know what it is," she said at last, "I know why my heart is on the breaking point this week. These crazy animals have explained it to me. Badger took care of poor Moley out of genuine affection just now, even though he'd been interrupted late at night during a storm in the middle of his sleeping season. That's it; I want to live that kind of life. I wanna be your Badger, Honey," she said to Philip. "I want you to be that for me. This is what I want for Christmas, and I only just realized it."

Philip opened his mouth to respond, but she raised her hand to stop him, and she went on. "I mean, I know we're going to church tomorrow and everything, but to me, I've got all I need right here tonight. What I'm searching for is connected to how we take care of each other, not just each other right here," she said drawing a circle around us in the air, "but each other in the larger sense; each other in society. I love how you set aside gifts for the poor," she said to Mark and me. "And oh gosh, I don't know. I think I've just seen too many mean and selfish people leaving broken marriages," she said. "I think my heart had grown coarse and hardened. But here are these animals, Ratty and Moley and the good Badger, all taking care of each other." A moment of silence crept into the room, but she wasn't quite finished. "And here we are, the four of us, sharing meals and stories and all this love." She choked up on this last phrase and wiped a tear from her eye, then she put her hands in her lap, and we could see her shoulders relax.

A long silence followed again as her final word hung in the air. A carol was playing quietly in the background. Philip put his arm around her and pulled her in close. "I'm sorry," she said at last. "I know it's Christmas and all, but something broke loose in here," pointing to her heart. "I only just realized now that love and care are enough. They're what we've got in our hearts—Philip, you and me, and these two great guys—it's about love. Love is the only thing that can save us in the end. Only love." She had talked it out, and we could see that she had come to the end of her thoughts and feelings.

"Well, then, here's to love," Mark proposed a toast. Four glasses went up together, and four friends toasted love.

After a moment, she passed the book to Mark, and we resumed the story. The animals shared a friendly supper which rendered conversation among them impossible for a long time, according to the text. Finally, when they could talk again, it was, unfortunately, only with a mouth full of food. Very sweet. After supper, Moley, Ratty, and Badger sat talking by the fire late into the evening, but soon they began nodding off. Good old Badger chased them both off to bed in his guest room which "smelt beautifully of lavender." Within thirty seconds, they were asleep.

In the morning, the Otter made an appearance. He had come to Badger's house looking for his friends from the Riverbank. There had been a lot of commotion back home, he told them, when both Moley and Ratty both went missing. Otter came here because he knew the Badger would help. And sure enough, after a generous breakfast in Badger's kitchen, he led them down a long passageway and bid them farewell as they emerged at last on the edge of the Wild Wood. They surveyed the countryside surrounding them and saw the Wild Wood behind them at last.

Then they began their final trek home to the Riverbank where they knew they'd be greeted by the river with its familiar and trusted voice.

We put the book down and cleaned up the room a little, tucking gift wrap into the recycle bin and turning off the music. There remained only the candles, the fire, and us. Christmas Eve was coming to a close in our cottage, but we all sat by the fire and talked for quite a while that evening. Soon, though, we, too, began nodding off, and we all went to bed. We could hear Philip and Claire whispering and giggling in their room late into the night. Mark and I cuddled and talked quietly about "the storms" in our own lives from which we had been saved. As we finally fell asleep, we had the sense that we had indeed come in from some blizzard and had found shelter here.

"Goodnight, Moley," Mark said.

"Goodnight, Ratty."

Chapter 16

Long Winter's Nap & the Feast

We awoke quite early on Christmas morning to the smell of Cornish sausage cooking somewhere nearby. It took us a few minutes to realize that the smell was coming from our kitchen right there in the cottage, and not from any other place. The local Cornish sausage—seasoned with fresh sage—has a distinctive flavor and smell, and we'd know it anywhere. As we descended the stair, we could also smell the coffee. And sure enough, there in the kitchen was Philip in a Santa hat, feeling very cheery. He had just poured a French press, so the coffee was hot. Carols were playing, and a stove full of food awaited us. He had mushrooms sautéing in a small pan, rashers of bacon under the grill, toast in the cozy, and eggs ready to scramble as soon as we were ready to eat. And of course, there was a pan of browned Cornish sausage.

Cornish sausage is made from beef, pork, and veal in equal parts. To that one adds about one-sixth as much bread crumbs mixed with lemon, salt, and a pinch of summer savory, thyme, and nutmeg. Chop half a dozen fresh sage leaves and sauté them briefly in light oil—and briefly means briefly. Toss them in, salt as you like, and mix. Voila! If you don't stuff this into casings, just keep it chilled until you use it. Philip had not made these sausages but bought them from the local butcher, who did make them in their own kitchen.

Good grief. You'd think that all we did for the week in St Ives was eat. We did do other things. We shopped, we slept, we looked at art, and we wandered the coastline—but we did do a lot of eating, that's true. We'd been up quite late on Christmas Eve as I mentioned: talking and waiting for Santa to appear. And, in a certain way, he did join us, but only because a group of local youth had come by, caroling their way through town while we were having our last glass of Port, and one of them had dressed up as...well, let's just say that Santa was with them. But it was now Christmas morning, and Philip was determined to get us off to a good start as he stood there grinning proudly over his stove.

"Who needs coffee?"

"Well, don't you look just like Mr. Badger," Mark said. "I'll take some of that coffee." So, standing there in the kitchen on Christmas morning, feeling for all the world like we were Moley and Ratty in Badger's kitchen, we had cups of strong coffee topped with double cream.

Claire came into the kitchen last, took one look at Santa Philip, and giggled. "What's going on?" She was still a bit bleary-eyed. "Just let me have a cup of coffee first," she said. And then to Philip: "How long have you been up, Honey?" The answer was on the stove. "And where did you get that hat?"

"Crack!" Mark and Philip pulled open the first Christmas cracker of the day. To properly discharge a cracker, two people are required, one on each end. Out popped a silly hat and an even sillier joke: "What does Santa like to do in the garden?" Mark asked. We all looked stumped. "Hoe. Hoe. Hoe." Mark finished. Groans. "And I'm not talking about the Andrews' Sisters," he improvised. More groans. Then he slipped on his paper hat, making him look like Jughead. It was Christmas morning, and we were all just a little goofy.

While Philip put the finishing touches on breakfast, Mark and I started fiddling with the oven. Mark had taken the rib roast out of the fridge so it would come up to room temperature before cooking which the recipe insisted was essential. We hadn't even had breakfast yet, so it seemed a bit early to me to get started on supper, but I was just the sous chef. British ovens have a life all their own with dials and cranks and little symbols that we always struggle to understand. We were standing by the stove, iPhone in hand, searching online for the various symbols for the controls on this oven, but we could find nothing helpful.

Mark was following a recipe for the rib roast which we'd never used before, but which someone had promised him was an excellent method and, as he told us, these people "love to cook." Loving to cook seemed like questionable credentials to me, but did

I mention that I was only the sous chef? The recipe involved cooking the roast at a very high oven temperature but only for five minutes per pound which, in this case, would be just thirty minutes. Yes, just five minutes. Then we were supposed to turn the oven off and not open the door for any reason whatsoever for at least two (and more like three) hours. If the house had caught fire, we would have left the roast behind. Even Bill, the butcher, had endorsed this method when Mark described it to him, so that was the plan. However, this only works if the oven can be turned on and warmed up first which we were unable to get it to do. We thought something might have been wrong with the timer, so we were monkeying around with that, turning it first this way and then that way, all to no avail. Now mind you, this was all rehearsal. It was much too early to cook that roast, but chefs like to make sure their equipment is working.

We interrupted the oven commotion for Philip's sumptuous breakfast. There's a long history in England of what is known as "a full English breakfast." It involves at least two kinds of meat, in this case, those rashers of bacon and the sausage, roasted tomatoes, sautéed small mushrooms, eggs, toast, and often baked beans, various puddings, and other items. No one could eat this every day and survive past forty years old; it's heart-stopping.

After breakfast, while they cleaned up, Mark and I returned to the oven timer. There was no one we could call for help; it was Christmas morning, for heaven's sake, and nothing online to explain it. Hmmm…stumped. We had a little time today before we were at the absolute deadline for this so, we did what seemed like our only option: we shoved the roast back into the fridge, gave up, and went to Christmas Mass. Dinner would be a bit later in the day than we had planned.

The four of us trundled ourselves down the Digey and onto Fore Street toward St Ia's. Construction on the parish church here began in 1410, and they finished building it in 1434, which is fifty-eight years *before* Columbus made his first voyage. It's ancient. It's dedicated, of course, to St Ia, the Virgin, as I've already said. They built the eighty-foot tower from huge Cornish granite slabs mined near Zennor and transported by sea to this site. I can't imagine how they could have maneuvered these slabs into place, much less lifted them up to the top of the tower. It was in an age before gas engines and machines. Truly remarkable to see. The builders also added grinning gargoyles to guard the perimeter, and these are most likely from the 15th-century.

The builders designed one of the aisles in the church for fishing families; it has plain glass in the windows so they could keep watch over their boats in the harbor. The baptistry is behind this "fishermen's aisle" and has carvings in the granite which are meant to remind people that baptism casts out demons. A close inspection of these creatures shows that they are not for the faint of heart.

The reredos on the back wall above the high altar is carved alabaster. On the right stands the patroness, St Ia. On the south aisle is that Lady Chapel which was added by the Trenwith family in about 1450 or so. It's in this chapel that Barbara Hepworth installed the memorial to her son, Paul.

You never know what you might find when you show up as a stranger in an established congregation, but it turned out that we

161

weren't the only strangers there that morning. The place was packed! Gratefully, the music was in a key we could all sing, the woman who gave the homily made a lot of sense, and the whole experience left us feeling cheery and buoyed. Churches and bars are some of the last places in our culture where people actually sing out loud in public. It's one of the elements of Sunday worship that I like the best. Even some of the old hymns, when sung by a crowd, can come to life again. But we had plans for after church on this Christmas morning so, as after the postlude concluded, we quickly departed.

Since dinner would be delayed, we decided to stop at one of the local surf shops to check their daily posting and figure out today's tides; we planned to visit Godrevy and the seal beach near there. This is the place that inspired Virginia Woolf in her 1927 novel about holidays at the sea, *To the Lighthouse.* The novel is obsessed with philosophical questions and actually takes place at the Isle of Skye, but it was her childhood visits to St Ives that formed the basis of the story and her ruminations.

Mark and I had made this plan at the last minute because the weather was favorable and we thought a substantial hike would do us all good. But, of course, when we stopped to check the tides, Claire and Philip weren't sure why. "Please don't tell me we're going to surfing school," Claire said.

"Surfing school!? Are you bloody nuts? We'd all die out there. Bill can't even swim. No, we're going to visit a bunch of grey seals."

"Gay seals? Who cares what seals do in private? And anyway, I don't think they're called a "bunch" of seals. I think it might be a "pod" of seals, or maybe a…well, I'm not sure."

"Actually," Mark said—and he somehow knows about these things—"you can call then a bob, a harem, a herd, a pod, or a rookery. Take your pick. I think on land they are called a colony, but when they're at sea, most people call them a harem, I'm pretty sure. We're spending Christmas Day with a harem of grey seals. Why not?"

We knew that the timing for this seal expedition was crucial; we'd have to arrive during low tide if we were going to see these guys. During the high tides, they all scoot out into the sea to have their lunch. We left the church about 11:30, and low tide was on the charts for 1:43 PM, so we had just enough time. We got ourselves organized and headed over to Godrevy and its lighthouse which is on the north end of St Ives Bay. We drove out of St Ives on the A3074 past Carbis Bay and on toward the A30, but at the Hayle roundabout, we hopped onto the B3301. We knew that if we followed this road, it would take us to Mutton Cove and the seals. There is almost always a colony of seals here at any time of year, but in the winter months, the numbers are more substantial, as many as a hundred. We were excited.

We drove past the car park at the National Trust office at Godrevy, went up the road a little farther, and parked in what folks call a "lay-by" which is a small, informal parking area that many local people use. Two or three other cars were also there, so we felt confident we had found the place. From the lay-by we continued walking up the road on foot and, where other walkers had worn a path, we made a right turn up a hill and across a field. It was a vigorous hike. Soon we reached the cliff top which looks down onto Mutton Cove quite far below—and there we should find the seals. We knew we were in the right place because other seal watchers were there with large cameras and field glasses. We had learned that the seals are sensitive to noise, so, like everyone else, we approached the place quietly. The whole hillside and cliff were as silent as a library; the only sounds came from the waves meeting the beach.

And there were seals, indeed, a large colony of them, mainly laying in the sun quite motionless, apparently digesting their fishy breakfasts. However, whenever one of them decided that he or she liked another spot better, even though already occupied by a fellow perfectly contented seal, a small commotion ensued as the two of them negotiated for that spot on the sand. Flappers flapped and, we imagined, some manner of seal cussing occurred. Then they'd all settle down again until…well, this kept going on all the while we watched. One seal after another decided it wanted some other seal's spot in the sun. In this way they reminded us of people: the grass is always greener, or in this case, the sand is always warmer, on the other side of the beach.

As we left them to their cove and their sand, we are agreed that they were indeed a harem of gay seals! Afterward, we walked around to the east side of the point and along back past the island and lighthouse. Eventually, we came to a rolling grassy sheep pasture with great views, so we paused and sat down to take it all in. This lighthouse was built in 1858 to mark the reef which has been a hazard to sailors for centuries. Just four years before that, in 1854, a ship and forty crew members were lost to these rocks. A local master mariner from St Ives called Richard Short wrote to the editor of the Shipping and Mercantile Gazette that year pleading for a lighthouse. In part, his letter made this dramatic appeal: "Scarcely a month passes by in the winter season without some vessel striking on these rocks, and hundreds of poor fellows have perished there in dark, dreary nights without one being left to tell the tale." They built the lighthouse a few years later.

At this point, each of us had had enough. The fresh air, our late nights, this vigorous walk, a little bit of existential angst, and the cumulative effect of many excellent meals all combined to create a "must have a nap" syndrome among us all. We drove back to St Ives almost in silence, each of us a bit wearier than the other. In fact, I dropped them near the cottage and let them walk home, then drove over to the car park alone. I savored my slow walk back and, by the time I got to the cottage, Mark was already sound asleep in his "long winter's nap." There was silence in Claire and Philip's room. I lay down quietly on the couch by the fire, pulled up a blanket, and was soon off to dreamland myself.

I could smell in the house, though, that Mark had finally had success with the oven. When he got back to the cottage, he explained later, he was still turning and cranking the dials around at random when suddenly and without any reason he could decipher, the oven came on. The heat rose quickly to 200 Celsius. He had heat at last, so he promptly opened the door and shoved in the roast. Then he went off to his nap. The beef, garlic, and rosemary were cooking, no doubt about that, and they smelled heavenly. He needed thirty minutes at that heat and, at precisely thirty minutes, the oven beeped and turned itself off. Now came the part where you don't open the oven door for any reason for the next three hours.

For the entire remainder of our time in the cottage that week, we never got the oven on again. We tried to repeat what Mark had done but got nothing. Somehow, for the sake of that lone standing rib roast over which I had worried so much, the oven agreed to help us celebrate the holiday. It was a Christmas miracle!

Those naps were the second Christmas miracle. Oh, my goodness. We slowly came out of our mid-winter slumber, showered, and got ready for Christmas dinner. Mark gave his parents a quick phone call to wish them a cheery holiday. His parents were in their early nineties then and still in their own home in St Paul. My family had gathered before the holiday for our annual Yule Log party in my hometown in Minnesota, so we had just seen them all. Philip was downstairs in the living room, sending email greetings to friends and neighbors. I chose some loungy, jazzy Christmas music for the evening and went to work on the table setting. We had decided that there would be no pre-prandial today; all our courses would be at the table itself. Besides, we had cookin' to do!

Mark took the lead now and assigned tasks to each of his three sous chefs. He appointed Claire the job of getting the brussels sprouts ready. Since we could not, under any conditions, open the oven, they'd require stovetop preparation. She cleaned them and cut a cross shape through their necks to allow the slightly bitter juices to cook out. Then she boiled and drained them, preparing to finish them just before the meal with butter and garlic and a dash of freshly minced rosemary. The brussels sprouts were sold on their stem, fresh from a local farmer, and the taste was exceptional.

Mark and I had gone out on an "herb run" earlier. Rosemary is common in this climate, and we know where to find the best "public" rosemary bushes in town. It's an evergreen shrub, and it's used here as a border plant along gardens or walkways, so it's abundant. It has very fragrant needle-like leaves that are best when chiffonaded to release more flavor, but on lamb or beef, it can be added whole and allowed to cook with the meat. As we started to prep the meal, a large bunch of rosemary lay waiting on the cutting board. We were hoping to find a patch of chives which Mark needed for one of his dishes, but we had to purchase that at the greengrocer.

We had also found—to our delight—a lovely patch of common mint, and it was a very public patch it seemed to us, so we harvested as much as we needed. Mint is a fantastically hardy herb that is easy to grow in the garden, but this wise gardener planted the mint in a well-contained patch. The problem with mint is that, once you plant it, you've got it for the rest of your life and it can spread to fill in any space. It mainly flowers in the summer, but it's readily available here in Cornwall all year round. Mark had a plan for something that required fresh mint, so this stood ready. Besides the herbs, we also had ready and waiting on the cupboard those brussels sprouts, carrots, and the potatoes that we had purchased at the farmers' market. It was shaping up to be a great feast.

Philip was responsible today for the carrots. He peeled and cleaned them, cutting them into thin rounds, which he steamed and chilled ahead of time to have ready when it was time to finish the dish. Meanwhile, he prepared his sauce with butter, a decent-sized pinch of fresh parsley, the rosemary of course, plus a pinch of two herbs he had brought with him: marjoram and oregano. At the last minute, he'd toss all of this into a sauté pan and finish it with salt and pepper. The marjoram is actually in the mint family, but it has sweeter pine and citrus flavors and is a stand-out in a vegetable dish like this.

Philip was also organizing the salad course. He had wisely prepared some beets to be baked along with the roast—wrapped in foil and sprinkled with a little olive oil—so when Mark got the oven to work, Philip was standing by to add his beets as well. Oven-roasted fresh beets are fabulous. He was ready to grab his packet of beets once Mark opened the over. He would then peel and slice them—still a little warm—on a bed of rocket. On top of the beets, he would spread chèvre which melts just a little, and on top of that, a small dollop of honey. Rocket, of course, is what the English call arugula. I used to think it was called rocket because it's a fiery tasting green and rocket sounds more fiery than arugula. But I have since learned that the word "rocket" actually evolved from the Italian word for the same plant, "ruchetta" as it worked its way over the Alps, across Europe, and into England. Most store-bought rocket is a bit bland tasting these days, but if you can find a back-yard gardener or good farmers' market, you'll be a convert to the fresh version. Philip got this batch at the local greengrocer, and it was excellent.

Mark put me to work on the potatoes, and here's where the goose fat came into play. I would typically use an oven for this recipe, so the range-top process was only a substitute. Once I had the potatoes cleaned (but not peeled) and the eyes removed, I cut them into two inch-sized pieces, roughly speaking. I cooked them by boiling them with rosemary—yes, we pinned the theme of this entire meal to rosemary—plus garlic and peppercorns, and then let them steam dry for a few minutes. If I had had an oven, I would only have par-cooked them at this point, but since I was going to finish them in a sauté pan, I had to cook them until fork tender.

To finish them—and mind you, Claire was at the same range with her brussels sprouts and Philip was there with his carrots—I joined the crowd at the stove and heated a couple large dollops of the goose fat in a large frying pan until very hot. Then I carefully laid the potatoes (along with the rosemary and garlic) into that fat and just let them sizzle, turning them as needed. Toward the end of this process, I gently squashed them, to create a little more surface which would make them extra crisp. The goose fat worked its usual miracle, and they turned golden and crunchy.

What happened next was Claire's fault. Did I mention that we were cooking with wine? None of us used any wine in the food, but the cooks were enjoying a sip here and there as a means of making sure the flavors were all correct. It seemed to be working. She still blames the wine for this.

Mark was busy getting an *au jus* put together and, as he passed her, she bopped him on the head playfully with a cooking spoon. Never one to let a head bop go unanswered, he stuck his finger into the butter dish and smeared a bit on Claire's chin. She squealed, and Philip started laughing, saying that may have been a mistake on Mark's part since Claire always tends to "win her big cases." Being the mother superior, I suggested maybe those two should behave themselves since we had three hot pans sizzling away on the range, but Claire, seeing an opportunity to make things worse, responded to my little scolding by rubbing a dab of the unused goose fat onto my glasses. Only Mark stopped us from an all-out food fight by finally opening that oven.

A long and reverent silence filled the room as the smell and look of that rib roast came into view. Mark took a sharp knife and cut into the end of the roast. Perfectly tender and medium rare—and it tasted like heaven. We were all back in focus now, and it was time to get this feast to the table, which we did without any further delay. The roast did not need to rest, as roasts usually do, because, as Philip pointed out in his chefly manner, it had been resting in that oven for three and a half hours. But Mark tented the roast anyway and slowed us down on our final finishing touches. We opened a bottle of Cava and went to the table which had been set and trimmed for the banquet. There we toasted the ghost of Christmas present, the saints who found this place, the nuns who were praying for it, the sea, the seals, the woman who had preached this morning, our fisherman's cottage, each other, and that damn oven, among other toastable people and places.

The meal lasted three hours. As the roast and our various side dishes rested a bit before serving, Mark surprised us with a perfectly prepared amuse-bouche of minty pea soup. People have been making pea soup for centuries. Nearly every western nation has some kind of pea soup history. Of course, England is pea soup's true homeland where it's made with mint and is a light and airy, sweet and delicate starter to any meal. The English version has within it the promise of summer soon to come. I'm sure that even the Queen loves it. In any case, this soup requires only about five minutes of prep time and fifteen of cooking time, and it's always best the day after you make it. Mark had found a minute when the kitchen was free and put it together for us yesterday while preparing his *Coquilles St Jacques*.

It's this simple: he sautéed an onion (it could also have been a shallot) in butter, added a suitable amount of veggie stock, and cooked local fresh peas (frozen would also work) in that liquid. Peas cook to tender within a few minutes so once cooked he removed them from the heat, added a handful of parsley and mint (more mint than parsley), along with salt and pepper and a tiny bit of cream. He blended that mixture with an immersion blender with which he travels the way some people never leave home without an umbrella. It's a good thing he had brought it since, as previously noted, there was no regular blender in this cottage. He served it with *crème fraiche* and sprinkled it with some of those fresh chives.

After the amuse-bouche, Philip served his salad, and with it, we finished off the Cava. I was the sommelier for the day, so next up was a Château d'Or et de Gueules 2015 La Bolida Mourvèdre from Costières de Nîmes, which is an area between the ancient city of Nîmes and the western Rhône delta, in the French department of the Gard. 2015 is a pretty young red, but I didn't have much choice in the wine store. We were in luck because this one, when allowed to have air for a few minutes, showed itself to have earthy notes filling the mouth with tannins, but also soft red fruit flavors—black cherry and tart mulberry. This roast, I knew, would have plenty of fat but no char since it was not being grilled. I knew we'd need a wine with some serious structure to it or it would have been lost in the rich flavors of the meat. I found two bottles of this wine at John's in St Ives, just a few steps down the street. It was affordable for a special feast, about $30.

The time had come now for the main course, but first, a short break for the final prep. While our wine breathed, Mark cut the meat between the ribs, and plated four lean and juicy pieces of prime rib. He added creamy horseradish sauce to the plate which we could scoop onto the meat, and he has a tasty au jus ready on the side. Claire and Philip piled the brussels sprouts on one end of a platter and the carrots on the other end. In between they garnished the platter with—you guessed it—a healthy sprig of rosemary. I put my goose-fat-cooked potatoes in a small bowl and poured a little of the remaining juice from the pan over them and, voila!

Our Christmas dinner was underway, but not without another toast. Our toasting during this week had become a pretty solemn ritual with us. We toasted the animal who gave its life for this meal, the farmers who raised the produce, our families back home, and the poor who would receive the equivalent sum of money we set aside. But then we went to work on the meal. We indeed were like that bunch of animal friends in Badger's house. We chatted and laughed. We told stories of conquests already accomplished and those about which we were dreaming. And we all expressed many ooohs and aaaahs about the food. The final toast of the meal came from Philip: "Here's to this fisherman's cottage and to having found a home in St Ives," he said. A steady chorus of amens all around the table.

After the meal, we agreed to head out for a short walk as a digestif, so we bundled up against the chilly early evening and tumbled down our stairs and out onto the Digey. We assembled ourselves, greeted passing neighbors, and headed toward the sea. Our walk took us down to Bumbles Tea Room where we turned right and headed up Back Road. Just past Penwith Gallery, we turned left onto Porthmeor Road and followed it to what is known locally as "the Island." Called initially *Pendinas* which means fortified headland, it's not actually an island at all but a short, grassy peninsula connected to the mainland by a narrow isthmus.

The whole place was buzzing with dogs and their owners, as well as dozens of other post-Christmas dinner walkers like us. The tide was out that afternoon, so the beach looked more expansive than ever. At the top of the Island stood the 15th-century Chapel of St Nicholas, which we thought would be a fitting destination on Christmas Day. The tiny chapel was restored in 1911 when they installed floor tiles depicting fishing scenes—they dedicated this chapel to mariners and their families—and the famous St Ives potter, Bernard Leach, created these tiles. The chapel is rarely open—we've never been inside it—and it's used now as a wedding and event venue, but only for a very small party of guests.

We walked around the lower edge of the Island returning full circle to the pathway that led back to town. We were all eager to get home to our cottage, slip into our jammies, and settle in front of the fire for the rest of the evening. The winter's early dusk was rapidly turning to darkness, so we picked up our pace a little, and soon we were back at our doorway.

Ratty and Moley were on our minds as we reassembled in the living room. Philip and Claire's dessert would come later, and they promised us a quintessentially British pudding experience.

Chapter 17
All This & Mary Berry Besides

We had left Moley and Ratty making swiftly for their Riverbank home after the experience of the Wild Wood and Mr. Badger's house. As the evening shadows came in, they realized they still had a long way to go before they reached their home. The two friends braced themselves for the last, long stretch through furrow and field. The Rat was walking ahead of the Mole, plodding along, thinking about supper and the warm fire that awaited them on the Riverbank.

Suddenly as they went along in the winter's early dusk, the Mole stopped in his tracks, his nose in the air, searching hither and thither in its efforts to recapture a strong sense, a smell, a memory that had hit him as he walked. We humans don't really understand animal noses. We have a sense of smell, but it's thin compared to that of an animal. Moley's nose was taking in the scents and familiar smells around him, but he was also becoming aware of an entire catalog of memories, all buried deep within his bones.

He stopped, smelled, nose in the air, sniff, sniff, sniff. Then, without warning and with a sudden jolt, it came to him: *Home!* He knew his old home, the one he had left that morning as he gave up on his spring cleaning, *must be near*. It was tugging at his heart and calling him. He had been so absorbed in his new life with Ratty and the river that he'd almost forgotten about his old home. It is certainly possible for someone to forget about one's home, but the truth is that our homes never forget about us. And now, his home was calling to him.

It was as clear as a bell to him. He had to return to his home. He called for Ratty, and he was full of real excitement. "Hold on!" he said, "Come back! I want you quick."

But the Rat dismissed him cheerfully, urging him to follow, still plodding along. Then the Mole called even more passionately, pleading with the Mole, and seeing him push onward, the Mole felt anguish in his heart. He begged again and again, but the Rat was by now quite far ahead of him and couldn't hear him. Ratty thought snow might be coming, and he wanted them safely in front of their fire before that happened. "We mustn't stop now, really!" he hollered back. Poor Mole, standing alone in the road, was heartbroken. A big sob was gathering. But Mole never questioned his friendship with Ratty, and he tore himself away from his desires to go home and caught up with the Rat who continued to march along, chatting cheerfully. Finally, the Rat sensed that the Mole's heart was not in this friendly banter, so he asked the Mole if something was wrong. It was then that the sobs came surging forth, first one, then another, and at last the Mole gave up and wept openly and freely. The Rat was astonished at this and, when a moment allowed it, asked him what on earth was wrong.

The Mole, choking on his tears, came out with the story all in one big rush of emotions. He knew his old home was not much of a place, but he loved it, and he had smelled it, and he wanted to go there, and when he called the Rat wouldn't turn back, and he had to leave it behind, and he thought his heart would break. All of this brought fresh waves of sorrow and homesickness. Sobs!

Mark happened to be reading at this point in the story, but he choked up so thoroughly that he handed me the book. Mark is a very tender-hearted guy. He wasn't so choked up about Moley's home as about his sadness. Mark tends to give his heart to anyone in trouble or pain. He has always given it to me that way. I've often said that Mark has taught me about compassion in ways I didn't even know I needed to learn simply by letting his own heart be what guides him.

I read onward. The Rat, meanwhile, stood there staring straight ahead. Then he reached out to the Mole very gently and said, "I see it all now. What a PIG I have been. A pig—that's me! Just a pig—a plain pig!" And then they started out again, walking more briskly along, but they weren't heading to the river. Where are you going? the Mole asked him. And the Rat answered that they were going to find Mole's home and that Moley should show him the way. Off they went.

And at this point in the story, as the two animals made their way to Mole's house, Philip announced that the time for their dessert had arrived. He and Claire just needed a few minutes in the kitchen for the final prep, so Mark and I sat by the fire and talked about our homes. For us, home is wherever the other one is. Like many of our contemporaries, we've moved more than once, leaving behind the people and places we once called home. At the moment, our home was our little farm north of the Twin Cities, but we both knew—and had been discussing the idea seriously—that it was nearly time to change. We didn't think growing old in such an isolated place would be for us. We missed the city. We had tended to my own dad's death a few years before this, and now it was time for us to help Mark's parents as they entered the end game of their lives. So home? We tend to take it with us, as long as we're together.

But dessert? Ah, the moment was upon us, so we made our way back into the dining room. They had turned the lights low and ushered us in as though we were entering a chapel. There on the table stood an impossible wonder. It was a round cake about five inches high covered with perfectly white and fluffy icing and topped with a tiny pine branch and red ribbons. "Where did this come from?" we wondered aloud. We'd been with this couple since we all landed. But here in front of us was a genuine, English Christmas Cake.

"Did you buy this?" I asked.

"Nope."

"So, this explains the hatbox," Mark said.

"Yes, it does indeed," Philip and Claire were both grinning widely. They had decided to use Mary Berry's recipe, of all things, which they'd seen on The Great British Bakeoff on PBS. They got a head start by actually baking the thing on what the Brits call "Stir-up Sunday" which is the last Sunday before Advent, the traditional day for English bakers to get their Christmas cakes underway. Who knew? Without giving away his secrets—or Mary Berry's—he simply explained it as a spicy cake, darkened with black treacle, and filled with fruits of various kinds. It's almost a fruitcake but not quite. It's baked in a round pan, cooled, and "fed" a little brandy every fortnight.

They had carried this booze-soaked thing all the way from St Paul to St Ives without once dropping it. Thank goodness the "hatbox" fit into the overhead bin on the plane, or there could have been a riot on board. We were traveling mainly with British folks heading home for their holidays, and a Christmas cake would have been just the thing. They tucked it into the car with their luggage, carefully carrying it into the B & B the first night. Then they brought it here and kept it in their room until yesterday, they told us.

While we were all out shopping yesterday and Philip had the kitchen to himself, he rolled out a large sheet of marzipan and used it to cover the cake. Marzipan is a thick paste made from almonds, sugar, and whole eggs. It rolls out like a pie crust and, as he explained, once he had it rolled, he lifted it carefully over the cake and laid it down very gently like a towel over a teapot. Then he whipped up some "royal frosting" and finished it. He had to get this done the day before we ate it so the frosting could harden a little. Then he tucked this whole thing into the bottom cupboard next to the glassware, covered it as well as he could, and hoped no one (or any other creature which might be stirring in the house) would find it before today. It was gorgeous.

We listened to this whole explanation—Philip and Claire were eager for us to finally see this—and then Mark said, "Well, guys, this is absolutely stunning. Totally unexpected. I just have one question, though. Black treacle? Isn't that intestines and stuff?"

"You're thinking of offal. We didn't use any internal organs in the making of this cake, trust me. Treacle is more like molasses; it's the stuff that's left over at the bottom of the barrel when they refine sugar."

"Wait. How do you know that?" Claire asked. "I don't get how you and Mark know so much about everything. It makes me nervous."

"Internal organs make me nervous," Mark said, "but the bottom of the sugar barrel doesn't sound that much better."

"Trust me."

"Do we have to sing or anything, or can we just cut into this beauty?" I asked. Meanwhile, Claire had visited John's Spirits down on Fore Street (which is just a few doors from that Methodist church) and found a bottle of wine from Cornwall—new to us— and was opening it. It was called Mena Hweg (which is Cornish for "sweet mountain") from the Knightor Winery which is a working winery at Trethurgy, near St Austell Bay. It's only ten minutes or so off the A30, smack in the middle of Cornwall between the beautiful villages of Trethurgy and Treverbyn. This wine was remarkable. It was a pale and semi-sweet wine, with aromas of floral and peach. There was a sense of light citrus (lime, maybe?) on the palate. The finish was quick. It wasn't a dessert wine, strictly speaking, but it paired very well with this cake.

As we sat once again around our table, the Christmas cake in the center and Nat King Cole crooning away from his Christmas album, I saw Philip raise his glass for a toast. 'Was there really anything left to toast?' I wondered to myself. 'Good grief. We've been toasting for a week already.'

"I give you Mark and Bill," he said, "the Founders of the Feast. Thank you, guys, for inviting us here and making this a shared journey. I never once felt like I was merely your guest this week but only that we were all genuinely finding our way together. St Ives is your little piece of paradise and thanks for including us."

"Thank you, Philip, and thank you, Claire," Mark said, tipping his glass to each. "This bit of paradise belongs to all of us, doesn't it? It's only paradise because we share it. No one can ownify this; it's not ownifyable. It's only sharifyable. If we kept it all for ourselves, private and selfish, it would become hell."

"Are those even words?"

"I made them up. Can we eat this cake now?"

We settled in for Christmas cake and Mena Hweg, savoring every bite and swallow. Travel with friends can be awful sometimes, but we four paired as well as the wines we chose paired with our meals. Somehow as we learned each other's histories and secret struggles, we grew closer. We grew to understand each other more. I would have to say that a genuine intimacy emerged among us and somehow our friends on the Riverbank fit into that.

Soon we were finishing tonight's story where Mole had brought Ratty to see his old home. When Mole arrived at his house, he saw that it had been unattended since he left: there was dust everywhere, and the room felt cheerless and deserted, worn and shabby. Oh, Ratty, he said with pain in his voice, I should never have brought you here. By this time, you could have been at home with your feet up, but now here we are in this dismal place.

But true to his character once again, the Rat paid no attention to this protest. He was busy running here and there, examining cupboards and closets and exclaiming about what a lovely home this was indeed. He lit a fire, put a duster into Mole's hand, and inspired his companion to cheer up. Soon there were visitors, including a chorus of field mice singing carols, an excellent meal, and that roaring fire. When they finally tucked in for the night, the Mole knew in his heart that he didn't want to give up the sunshine and fresh air of the river, but that it was wonderful to have this place to call his own. Home sweet home, indeed. Dulce domum, as we say in Latin.

At this point, Mark was "resting his eyes," and Philip was nodding off. We had early plans for Boxing Day so we should have gone off to bed, but I said, "I'm just going to have one more tiny piece of that cake. I can't stand the thought that it's all alone in the kitchen."

An hour later we were still sitting by the fire, chatting and nibbling and sipping. We were all wide awake again. 'What's wrong with us?' I thought. The truth was that we were lingering because we didn't want this day to end: Philip's breakfast, that friendly crowd in the parish church, those goofy grey seals, those long naps, that lovely feast at our Christmas supper, the sweet coming home of Mole and Rat—all that and Mary Berry besides.

Chapter 18
Padstow & Your Inner Toad

The first stop on our road to Padstow was Starbucks. Yes, Starbucks, the American coffee people. St Ives is a place entirely without American or even British fast food, so you have to drive out of town to find it. We had just two days left here in Cornwall, so maybe we were taking a tiny step toward re-entering our former lives. Earlier that morning we had to decide whether to drive the colorful, slow coastal road to Padstow or to head quickly up the A30 to Three Burrows and the A3075. At first, it seemed we were choosing the former until I mentioned that there's a Starbucks at the traffic circle at Three Burrows, and then the latter route won the vote, 3-1.

So, a skinny white chocolate mocha won the day and Philip's heart. I think he'd been longing for one of these all week. Fortified with coffee, tea, and of course, a biscuit or two, we drove north along the A3075 through towns with poetic names like Penhallow and Goohavern to Newquay. From there we followed the A392 past Quintrell Downs and White Cross to the A39 which took us all the way north, through Winnard's Perch to the B3274 which delivered us on time to Padstow.

We had decided to spend Boxing Day there and to get there in time for the Mummers' Day Parade. In much of England, most pubs and shops are closed on Boxing Day. We once had to beg for supper from the owners of a bed and breakfast just outside Gatwick Airport because we didn't know that we couldn't find supper anywhere on December 26. On another visit here, we pumped gasoline into the tank of a car with a diesel engine. On Boxing Day, no less. What a mess.

In Britain, according to the stories they tell now, it was a custom for servants or tradesmen to collect "Christmas boxes" on the day after Christmas, December 26, the Feast of St Stephen. It was to thank them for their services throughout the year. And often these servants or publicans and shopkeepers had spent Christmas Day itself serving the rich, so the day after Christmas was one on which the rich indirectly served the servants, at least a little. And the servants and shopkeepers would also be free on Boxing Day to go and see their own families after Christmas, presumably carrying with them a box of gifts, money, and even leftover food. In any case, many shops and pubs close down on the day after Christmas.

But Padstow is wide open and for a long time has celebrated Boxing Day with a Mummers' Parade. Mummers' Day is sometimes also called "Darkie Day," but it's not a reference to people with dark skin. It very well may be a reference to people who worked in the many mines that Poldark has now made famous throughout Cornwall. In fact, it's sometimes known as Darking Day. It's an ancient Cornish midwinter celebration, and it was once part of the pagan heritage of solstice events that were a large part of Cornish culture. In these events, people would do what's called "guise dancing." To succeed at guise dancing, one had to, well, *disguise* him or herself, and this often meant painting their faces dark or wearing masks. There are similar and more extensive celebrations in the springtime in various parts of Cornwall, including here in Padstow.

Another reason that guise dancing was popular was that it hid the identity of the dancer. This would allow someone to perform outlandishly without having to face people at the water cooler the day after the office party.

In any case, we drove ourselves right into the heart of Padstow taking the B3276 down the hill past the big Metropole Hotel, down onto Riverside where there are two public car parks. We found a space in one, paid for our ticket and put it back in the windshield, and walked a block or two into the harbor. By the time we got there, the town was buzzing, and it was only 11 AM. We aren't sure what time the parade started because it seemed to follow no particular route but instead simply wandered around the center of town. It was made up of a loose crowd of mummers preceded by a somewhat boozy sounding—and looking—accordion band, dressed up in quite a snappy manner with hats and garlands. Very festive.

There was a crowd of people in the streets, and everyone seemed to be having a terrific time, so we joined in. We followed the parade for a while, keeping out of its way as well as we could. It led us into Middle Street on which we found an attractive old building with an arched entry that we guessed may have been a poorhouse in its day. It was located kitty-corner across the street from one of Rick Stein's cafes. It's hard to visit Padstow and not notice the presence of Rick Stein. Since lunch was our next order of business anyway, we decided to tour the culinary scene in town and make a choice. Rick Stein's was first.

Stein is an English celebrity chef, restaurateur, and television personality. Early in his life he and a friend converted a local disco into a nightclub right here in Padstow. At first, things went well for them, but frequent brawls with local fisherman and other problems caused the police to shut the place down. Not an auspicious beginning for Stein. But since they still had a license for a restaurant in town and they were facing bankruptcy, they tried again with Stein running the kitchen this time, using his experience as a trained chef. In time this became what is now the Seafood Restaurant. That first success grew into a small empire here including a bistro, a café, a patisserie shop, a gift shop, and a cooking school. As I said, it's hard not to notice Rick Stein here.

The restaurant on Middle Street is called Rick Stein's Café. This location also offers lodging, as do at least five other of Stein's fooderies, both here in Padstow as well as in some other villages nearby. This Café is open for three meals per day, and the menu is eclectic. It includes chicken noodle soup which the chef serves as a main course at dinner, rump steak, mussels, sea bass, and hake, as well as a dish called meen kulambu, which is a fish curry dish from southern India. See what I mean? Eclectic.

Besides the flagship Seafood Restaurant and the Café that we were visiting, Stein also owns or has an interest in many other locations in Padstow. He owns St Petroc's Bistro and Ruby's Bar next door to it, Stein Fish and Chips, and a place called Fisheries and Seafood Bar which, among other features, has working fishmongers.

It seemed to us that Stein's influence here, although significant, only helped stimulate other restaurateurs and guest house owners. This town is bustling with places to eat, and it's clear that tourism has replaced fishing as the primary local industry. In the end, we chose the Harbor Inn, which Stein does not own but which is a pub with lots of local beers. They welcome dogs, families, and apparently, mummers since they all packed this place after the parade. We wanted a decent pub lunch with a pint or two to prime our pumps for shopping, and we got what we wanted.

After lunch, we headed back toward the center of town on the South Quay and followed the streets around into the shopping district. A lot of shops were open, and we crawled through at least a dozen. Packages were slowly starting to appear on our arms as we snapped up post-holiday bargains. A sweater here, a pull-over there. Claire bought some locally made soap. Mark bought a running shirt. I wasn't shopping as much as looking, but I did decide to honor Rick Stein just a little, so I popped into his patisserie and indulged myself in an utterly sinful and sumptuous slab of chocolate-covered honeycomb. I had to find a restroom afterward to wash up; it was that good.

An hour of shopping is always enough so soon we were looking toward the road home. Besides, we doubted that we could stuff even the few things we were buying into our already-overpacked luggage for the trip back to St Paul. No need to worry about the honeycomb in that regard!

We took the short route home from Padstow and, once we got there, it was all about beef and barley soup made with leftovers from yesterday's holiday meal. I drifted off to read a new book on art history which I'd gotten for Christmas. Philip was holed up in the living room, reading the parts of *Wind in the Willows* that we had chosen to skip. Claire was hanging with Mark in the kitchen, chatting about this or that. Soon they were serving the soup with crusty brown bread and Cornish butter along with a local ale called Skinners.

Skinners is brewed in Truro and was the ingenious idea of Philip and Sarah Skinner. They produce both cask and bottled beer, the latter of which was on our table. Their flagship ale, Betty Stogs, is the one that the fellow in the Tinners Arms had asked Claire about, but we were drinking what's known as Cornish Knocker which has also won prizes.

Knockers were tin-mine-dwelling guys who would go around knocking on the mine walls to lead miners to the richest seams. They apparently had an ear for good ore. Their only pay, as the story goes, was a portion of the pasties when the miners ate their lunch, or maybe also a sip of beer. Nowadays, they say knockers can occasionally be heard in local pubs, knocking on the bottles. Who knows?

"So, I have a question," Philip began as we finished the supper dishes. He was the philosopher, and there were always questions. He eyed Mark and me for a long moment. He had a very serious look on his face. We could feel the boom dropping. "Why haven't you told us about Mr. Toad?" He was almost accusatory in his tone, as though we had tried to keep secret something that should have been shared.

Why indeed? Mr. Toad is arguably the most popular and well-known character in *Wind in the Willows*, but because we knew we'd only have time to read about half the book during this journey, we decided to stick to Moley and Ratty, Badger and Otter. This left out some brilliant bits, though, and Philip had found one of them.

Mark's favorite chapter is "The Piper at the Gates of Dawn." In the story as Grahame tells it, we learn that one day, Portly—Otter's young son—turns up missing along the river. Moley and Ratty set out in earnest to help find him, sculling along the riverbank under the light of the moon. Among the night sounds they were—quite suddenly—able to hear a clear, distinct voice like that of a piper, calling them forward. Was it the wind in the willows? Or was it, yes, it must have been that divine force which gives life and light to the animals. It was the god, Pan, the patron of the wild, of all creatures great and small. The piping rose and fell as they followed it. Where was this piper? As they rowed up into a backwater, the sound became clearer. "This is the place of my song-dream, the place the music played to me," Rat whispered to Moley. "Here, in this holy place, here if anywhere, surely we shall find him."

Then, without any fear or panic, the animals fell into a state of awe, a wonderful and peaceful state. In that remarkable moment, the Rat responded to a call. He raised his head as the dawn began to break, and there, in the heart of that rich meadow, he looked up and found himself staring into the very eyes of the "Friend and Helper." Kindly eyes. Loving eyes. Gentle limbs. The shaggy limbs of the goat-god. The mighty form of Pan. And there, sleeping peacefully in his care was Portly, cradled by the Helper. As the morning sun broke upon them, suddenly—as quickly as it had begun—the vision left them. They helped young Portly back to his family, and there was joy along the bank. Mole and Rat experienced this encounter with the Friend, but at the same time, they also received the gift of forgetfulness, allowing them to appreciate the moment without having to understand it.

The piper appears in chapter seven of the book which we also did not read this week—and it's brilliant. But Mr. Toad? He was another story. We had a love-hate relationship with him. We had indeed named one of the buildings on our farm after him, a shed which we called Toad Hall. Toad's mansion in the story is called the same. And I suppose maybe we named the whole farm after him since it was known as Toad Hill. We chose that name—not to honor Mr. Toad—but because the farm had lots of toads on it. They'd been there before us, and we wanted to manage the land in such a way that they would still be there when we left. Lots of mulch. Not many chemicals. We made all those decisions with the toads in mind.

"Yeah," Claire chimed in, "so who's this Mr. Toad? Let's have the story, guys. What are you trying to hide?"

We weren't so much *hiding* Mr. Toad as *avoiding* him. But since they were asking, we decided to read one more chapter in the book. We had the evening before us, so why not? Claire was the first among us to read. This chapter opens, by coincidence, with Mole asking Ratty to introduce him to Mr. Toad, just as Claire and Philip had asked us. At the time, the Rat was composing a little ditty about the ducks in the river, and he was quite taken with his rhymes. The Mole less so. He had to pull Ratty away from that very important task. "I wanted to ask you," Mole said, "won't you take me to call on Mr. Toad? I've heard so much about him, and I do so want to make his acquaintance."

The Rat, being an affable fellow, agreed immediately and set himself to preparing the boat for a trip up the river toward Toad Hall. As they rounded a bend, Toad's house came into view, a large, dignified, old house set on an even larger lawn with stables, a boat-house, and a banqueting hall. "Toad is really rather rich, you know..." Rat informed his friend. They tied up their boat and walked up the lawn past glorious flower beds where they found old Toady resting in a wicker chair and looking at a large map.

"Sounds like you Claire," I said as she passed the book to Philip.

"Oh you," she said. "Just you wait. That map will come in handy; you'll see."

On seeing his friends, Toad was elated. He met the Mole with gusto, and Rat could see that Toad was up to something new. Toad, it seems had passed through one craze after another. He had been moving from one state of absolute certitude about the latest and the greatest fad to another. The most recent of these had been boating. So, the wise and wary Water Rat wondered what Toad might be up to now. But before all that, Toad had to boast, "Finest house on the whole river," he exclaimed to Mole. "Or anywhere else, for that matter," he couldn't help adding.

"Ugh," Philip said putting the book down in his lap, "sounds like a certain recent American president, doesn't he?" Boasting is something that always makes one look rather small even though the goal of a boast is to look large. Many of us have an "inner Toad," I suspect. We think of our work or family or garden as the best. We know how to do it, we tell ourselves, but those other fellows, what do they know? Toad did boast a lot, and he was self-centered and conceited. He did tend to override everyone in the group with his own willful desires. But, gosh, he must have possessed some redeeming qualities. I just can't think of any at the moment.

But back to our story. Rat inquired about his boating plans, but Toad interrupted, "Oh, pooh! Boating!" he said, "Silly boyish amusement... I've given that up...sheer waste of time."

And soon Rat and Mole learned about Toad's new passion, a caravan, a canary-yellow, gleaming, large, new, caravan. The Mole was excited, but the Rat wasn't amused. Still, at Toad's absolute insistence, the three of them set out on a journey down the road. The Rat began by insisting that he was not coming along, and that was that. But of course, in the end, he gave in. They all worked together to pack the wagon with onions, hams, baskets of bread, bottles of cider, and all the other needs they might have on "the open road." Catching the horse to draw this cart was another matter. The horse hadn't been consulted and preferred his paddock, but despite his annoyance, he was eventually harnessed to the caravan—and off they went down the dusty road.

The Rat missed his riverbank home, and Mole knew it. Mole knew that the Rat had gone along with this crazy journey only because he saw the Mole's excitement and didn't want to disappoint. As they tucked in for the first night, Mole "reached out from under his blankets, felt for Rat's paw in the darkness and gave it a squeeze. "I'll do whatever you like, Ratty," he whispered. "Shall we run away tomorrow morning quite early...?"

"No, no. We'll see it out," Rat answered.

But the following day as they journeyed along the road—Mole talking with the horse while Rat and Toady walked together behind the cart—there occurred an incident that would change the course of their lives. Behind them they saw a small cloud of dust and from its center came a vehicle full of energy, as if from outer space. As sit approached, they could hear it. "Poop, poop, poop," it went. Then it raced by them so swiftly and with such force that it scared the horse half to death. The whole operation—cart, horse, and all—crashed into the ditch. What was it, they all wondered? But it soon became clear that it was a smart, new, glass-covered *motor car*. For Mole and Rat this had been a disaster as the caravan had a broken wheel and the poor horse was inconsolable. They fell to work trying to fix this mess, but the Toad, entranced by this gleaming new motor car, sat in the middle of the road, legs out in front of him, staring after the dust cloud, muttering from time to time, "poop poop."

"You see?" Mark said. "This Toad is a difficult creature. It's all about him all the time. He has to be in the center of everything. He can't stand to let anyone else stand in the spotlight. I honestly don't like him very much."

And that brings us back to that "inner Toad" which we all have, I started saying. It's much easier to see this guy in other people's personalities than in our own, but it's possible for any of us to be willful and selfish just like Mr. Toad was. Sometimes when we feel strongly committed to a plan or desire or even just to our own tastes, we can easily—and without realizing it—override our mates. One of the lessons we can draw from a week spent together like the one we were about to conclude is that most small, daily decisions don't matter that much. There are almost always several good options. Being affable helps the whole group enjoy the time. Mr. Toad never understood this, I finished, and in him there is a lesson for us all.

"Well, I think he's darling," Claire weighed in at which point Philip just rolled his eyes and said, "Come on, Miss Toady, let's go to the pub." And off they went, providing Mark and me with a quiet evening alone.

Chapter 19
Trebah Garden

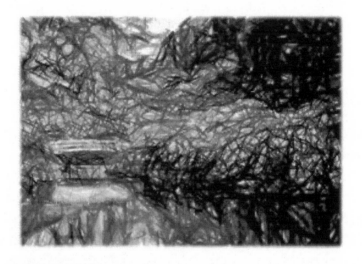

The following day—our last full day together in Cornwall—began with a journey.

Mark got out of the car and immediately, like Moley in the furrow with that scent he remembered, Mark had his nose in the air: Sniff, sniff, sniff. "There's jasmine blooming near us," he said, walking toward the edge of the car park and around the corner to the left. We all followed, and soon, sure enough, there it was, a winter-hardy planting of jasmine. "It's *Jasminum nudiflorum*," he announced.

Claire looked at me in bewilderment. "He has somehow learned the Latin names of most plants," I told her. "He's a sort of plant genius. I studied Latin for six years in school, but he speaks more of it than I do."

We were out on our last day in Cornwall, and we had decided to visit Trebah Garden for the afternoon. The climate on much of this peninsula means that winter gardens are beautiful and abundant. They're often subtropical and filled with unusual flora and fauna found nowhere else in England. There are twenty-nine gardens here in Cornwall alone and, of course, hundreds more throughout England. It is indeed a nation of gardeners. Some of these gardens remain open all winter, and today we had chosen Trebah.

We had driven out of St Ives to the south on the B3311 through Halsetown and across the peninsula toward Penzance and St Michael's Mount. St Michael's (not to be confused with Le Mont-Saint-Michel off the coast of Normandy) is a tidal island to which one can walk at low tide on a constructed causeway of rocks. The island is fifty-seven acres. For a long time, it was a Benedictine monastery, which is what it looks like with its steeples and towers standing at the top of the island with lush greenery all around. It's been here a very long time; the monks built the buildings at the top of the island in the 12th-century. Whoever owned it in 1659 sold the whole place to Colonel John St Aubyn. His descendants, known as the "Lords St Levan," still live there today. In 1954, the 3rd Baron St Levan donated almost all of the island to the National Trust. He also provided enough money to maintain the place. The St Aubyn family now has a 999-year lease, allowing them to live in the castle while they also help the public visit its historic rooms.

The sky was brilliant blue as we pulled into the parking lot, and the view of the Mount was stunning. We got there just in time to walk across the causeway and have a cup of tea in their café. The Mount was open for tours but, since the tides were not in our favor, we walked back to the mainland before high tide. Claire decided on the walk back that she'd like to be known as "The Lady St Paul," but we were doubtful that our friends at home would go along with her on this.

"Well, even if they don't," Claire said as we reached the car, "you guys can call me Lady Claire for the rest of the week here."

"OK, Lady Claire," I said, "get out that giant map of yours and let's find the road to Trebah. Or is a Lord not allowed to give orders to a Lady?"

"It depends on the order—and on the tone of your voice. And the tone I'm hearing doesn't sound like what a Lady wants to hear."

"OK, fine, my ladyship. What about the map?"

We knew we needed to be on the north side of the Helford River to find Trebah Garden, so we decided to follow the A394 all the way to Long Downs. From there we wiggled our way through a dizzying array of small roads and turns until we got to Mawnan Smith. It's a short drive from Mawnan on to Trebah Garden. It was in this parking lot that Mark caught the scent of jasmine.

Our first order of business after arriving at the garden, of course, was lunch in their dining room. The place was buzzing with winter visitors, and the smells and sounds of the entry building and gift shop were cheery. We ordered light lunches from their daily menu. Claire had the squash soup which was built on chicken stock and finished with a drop of truffle oil. Mark and I both tried the vegetable soup which, in keeping with how local cooks often present these soups, had been thoroughly blended into a thin porridge consistency. We couldn't make out any individual vegetables, but we knew we were tasting quite a bit of "swede," which is what the English call rutabaga. Philip had his way with their warm winter salad, made from roasted butternut squash, beetroot, leek, and avocado with a poached free-range egg and watercress. The bread was dark, crusty, and grainy.

After lunch, we headed for the garden. We followed what was called "the Lawn Path" down to the water garden where we dawdled a while to listen to the falling water. There's a natural spring here, and the water features run the full length of the ravine in which the garden is located. At the bottom of the ravine is the sea. From there we climbed up Stuart Hill to Badger's Walk mainly because we were all fans of Badger and wanted to walk on the lane named after him. This path took us along the west side of the garden, which covers some twenty-five acres. We passed along and above the rhododendron garden which, even in winter, was beautiful. Winters are light here, and the micro-clime in this ravine makes it possible to grow things that in other parts of Cornwall would not withstand the winter.

The history of Trebah is a fascinating tale. It was created in 1831 by a wealthy Quaker family from the area, Charles Fox and his brothers. They're all from Falmouth which is northeast of Trebah, and they made their money in mining and shipping. They've had a significant influence on many Cornish gardens, including this one but also Glendurgan, Penjerrick, and Rosehill. They're all filled with exotic plants and trees. Charles Fox and his brothers planted many of the trees and shrubs that we see in the garden today. They took meticulous care with the design of the footpaths and plantings.

Charles and Alice Hext owned the garden from 1907 to 1939. They significantly expanded the plantings and frequently opened it to the public. He was the High Sheriff of Cornwall, and they often hosted public events including one at which they entertained Edward VIII and Wallis Simpson before their marriage and his abdication in 1936.

Badger's Walk led us past at least six "champion trees," which are trees that are either taller or have more girth than any others in the country. This garden boasts nearly a dozen such trees. As we started down the hill, we passed a Giant Pink Tulip tree (*magnolia campbellii*, according to Mark), a Chilean Tepa tree, and a Japanese Yew, all champion trees and all magnificent. The path eventually dropped us onto the Davidia Walk at the Azolla Pool. We turned right and headed for the beach. On our way, we passed two stunning garden areas, the Gunnera Patch and the Hydrangea Valley.

Gunneras were new to all of us. They are native to places like Latin America, Australia, Hawaii, Southeast Asia, or Madagascar, so how they can raise them here in Cornwall is remarkable. The Latin name is *Gunnera manicata*, and it's often called Brazilian giant-rhubarb or "dinosaur food," a name which I think fits the plant. Its leaves were as big as four feet across, and a single plant can fill a space as big as ten by ten square feet. The underside of the leaves and the whole stalk had nasty-looking spikes on them. In the winter the garden caretakers cover the plant stems with their own giant leaves to protect them, creating the look of a field of small pup tents whose owners had abandoned them.

The Hydrangea Valley led to a small bridge and the Mallard Pond. Beyond that, we found the beach. During the second world war, Trebah's Polgwidden Beach was a departure point for the 29th US Infantry Division which sailed from this very place to make the terribly difficult D-Day assault landing on Omaha beach. The 29th was under the command of Major General Charles Hunter at the time of the invasion. They left this beach on June 6, 1944, carrying a large number of transport vehicles. The Germans had strongly fortified Omaha Beach, and the loss of life for this division was enormous. The seas were heavy on the day of the attack, the fighting was chaotic, some ships sailed off course because of the weather, and some, including the 29th, landed late in the day after commanders reorganized the attack plans. The 29th Division lost 2400 men in the Omaha Beach assault and battles that followed, but they pushed inland and soon began to gain ground and, of course, eventually were a crucial part of the Allies' victory.

As we stood on the beach that day, we thought of those young men, eighteen and nineteen years old, who had come here from the United States to fight against a terrible and violent political movement. They came to fight Nazi and Fascist ideas even though they were young and may not have fully understood the global and historical impact of their actions. Their sacrifice saved the world from an unimaginable terror. Their families' sacrifice was enormous, too. We stood there on that beach in full and fearless freedom because of them. It was a very moving and powerful moment for us all.

After the beach and our private memorial to the brave heroes of that war, we made our way back up along the other side of the ravine. We loved seeing the dogs in the garden, all well-mannered and all welcome. And because this was a holiday week, lots of children. Their laughter filled the ravine. On the way back, two more champion trees: a colossal Rhododendron and a Hiba tree, which I had never seen before. Hibas are conifers in the cypress family, according to Mark. This tree is Japanese in origin and is the source of treasured oils. The oil from this tree is fragrant and pale yellow. They extract it through a process which involves steam applied to the wood chips of the tree. It's in quite high demand, but there would be no wood chips made from this gorgeous—and protected—specimen.

After the war and until 1981 this garden fell into severe decline. It's hard to believe it as we stand here now, but the original estate was sold off as smaller parcels, and one of those was the house and garden. Between 1961 and 1971 Trebah was owned by the Cornish race car driver, Donald Healey. He improved the beach and restored the water features, but it wasn't until Trebah was purchased in 1981 by Major Philip Hibbert, a parachute regiment major and veteran of Arnhem, and his wife, Eira, that the fortunes of the garden took a turn for the better. They entered into an extended period of restoration, and in 1990 the Hibberts donated the house and garden to the Trebah Garden Trust where it is today.

Major Hibbert later gave an account to a local historical archivist regarding their decision to restore Trebah. The source for this account is unknown, but shortly after buying it, Major Hibbert had walked through his new property with Dr. Challiner Davies who may have been from the Royal Horticultural Society. There, under a dense canopy and over-grown forest, they found the remains of what had been one of England's most exquisite gardens until 1939. They are said to have gone back to the house "somewhat shaken" and poured a glass of gin. Dr. Davies turned to the Major and said something like, 'I do realize that you and your wife are not gardeners, but you now own an important property with a garden that you—or someone—could restore. If you don't restore it now, we may lose it forever. If you would agree to give up three years of your retirement and attend to this, you'll have a lovely view, and you can enjoy your gin on the terrace forever afterward.'

The Hibberts did, in the end, decide to give up "the first three years" of that retirement to restore the garden, but surely, they never dreamed that, instead of three, the project would take them a quarter-century. "The decision to do this," Major Hibbert eventually wrote, "has given us the happiest twenty-four years of our lives and, had we not taken up the challenge, we'd have been dead long ago of gin poisoning and boredom."

Gin poisoning aside, we were back near the main building now, but one last champion tree awaited us, a prehistoric-looking grove of wooly tree ferns, known in Latin, according to Mark, as *Dicksonia antarctica*. We were standing under the most famous tree fern in cultivation in the north, and it was a genuinely majestic plant! They have dense, dark brown trunks covered in overlapping frond stalk bases, sort of like a palm tree. From the top flow upward half a dozen or so huge fronds which are between three and five feet long, giving it a sturdy and lively look.

There's a story told about how Trebah Garden has survived so long because it has a soul that lures in owners and visitors alike. That must be what happened to Philip and Eira Hibbert. It positively enchanted and charmed us as we walked through it today. Now we strolled toward the main building, arm-in-arm, savoring the fragrances and colors. Our non-stop chatter as we walked through Trebah became silence as we walked toward the car park; our hearts were filled with appreciation for this beautiful place.

"Do you realize," Claire finally said, "that my phone has not made a sound in the last three days? Not even a beep. This phone has constantly been interrupting me for many years. It rang or beeped all day long, even after I retired. But here in this place, it has been rendered silent. And it was replaced with the sounds of wind in the willows, birds in this garden, and waves lapping against the shore. Sheer bliss."

Chapter 20
Our Last Supper

With our heads full of garden views and sights we had never seen before—and had not expected to see on that day—we started the journey back to St Ives and our final meal together. During the car ride home, Claire asked Mark about all those Latin names for plants that he knows, and about all the recipes he pulls out of his head, and about why he travels with a box of herbs and spices—not to mention an immersion blender—and about his painting. "Where did you learn how to paint so well," she asked him. "How do you know how to do all that?"

"I don't know," he said. "I pay attention to things. I look at plant leaves and know that if they're from the maple or Acer family, for example, they're almost always palmate and lobed, have opposite branching, and winged seeds. Box elders are in that family, and we have a lot of those at home, which we shouldn't have because they aren't native and they're weak trees." Claire looked at me as if to say, 'Does he always talk like this?'

"As for recipes," Mark went on, "Philip will agree, I think. They can help you construct the basics of a dish, but they can't put in the flavor or help you with a substitution if you need one or even help you finish and present the dish. You know, on Christmas we had no oven except for the roast, so we had to go a different way. What good would a recipe have done us?"

"Well, but what about people who don't cook," Claire protested. "What do they do?"

Philip answered. "They need to learn to cook. Listen he said, one thing I'm taking home with me from this week with these guys is that we—you and I Claire—we want to start having supper at home more often." Claire was listening. "These guys light candles on their table every darn night," he said. "Even with that bowl of beef soup the other night, we dined in candlelight. And it was soup with Sinatra tunes and red wine. Wow. Who lives like this?"

"I think you know," I chimed in, "that we are not among the idle rich. Most of our meals are very simple. But to add some candlelight, or to turn off the TV—anyone can do that. A meal is like a liturgy to us. It's sacred. It's where we talk and make most of our decisions. And as you know, it's where we meet our friends. Don't you agree that sharing a meal is very intimate? Just think of all the meals we had this week here. Wow.

"Honey," I said, turning to Mark, "could you please pull out a map? There must be some shortcuts that'll get us home."

Claire beat him to it, dug out her map, and started looking. "Where are we? Are we still in England?"

"Not for long, my dear," Philip answered her.

"Ohhh, I wanna stay. Can we, Philip? Let's stay here and never go home."

"Home calls you, Sweetie. Remember Moley? You can leave for a while, but it calls you back, back to your familiar and comfortable place. And besides, just think of all we're taking home with us. With you retired and around the house, we'll have a new lease on life. I'm kinda excited to get home."

"The map?" I asked. "We're on the A394, and we just passed Newtown." Philip was studying the map now and suggested we go all the way to the A30 and head over to the Hayle roundabout. Dusk was settling in, and it would be easier than finding our way on the small cross-country roads in the dark.

We did that. Back at our cottage, we all took turns in the shower, packed up a few things, and started getting ready to leave in the morning. "I'm going to have to check this bag," we heard Claire say across the hall in their room. "I had to unzip the fat bag expander. It'll never fit in the overhead bin." Mark went down and gathered his herbs and spices. I collected together the music and candles. We had a small piece of cheese, some leftover butter, and a few other things in the frig. We wrote a thank you card to the owners of the house and left them with a bottle of Prosecco for

New Year's. We set out what we needed a quick breakfast: coffee, tea, some bits of food, but we knew there was a Starbucks up the road at Three Hallows. We were moving home, one step at a time.

Once we had gathered in the living room, a teeny bit of sadness seemed to be emerging. We opened our last bottle of wine and poured a glass for each of us. Philip managed to pull together a small appetizer plate for us from whatever he found in the kitchen. We had lit the fire, but we had shifted from holiday carols to loungey jazz music. Except for those nuns for whom this was only the fourth day of Christmas, the holiday was behind us once again. Another year was about to roll in. No one wanted to say anything about the end of the week, but there we were.

We chatted about Trebah a while, about the Hibberts and how they had saved both Trebah and themselves at the same time. They thought what they wanted was to retire, drink gin, and never work again. But the universe had other energies floating around, and they ended up taking on a tremendous job, working at it for more than two decades, and loving it! "You see?" Claire said. "You never know what might show up on your pathway in life."

"I'm telling you," Philip said to her, "we've got a lot of new mail in our inbox."

"I just can't get those kids out of my mind, the ones who boarded those ships in 1944. Did they have any idea what they were getting into that day? Did they know that, for many of them, it would be their last morning alive? I wonder if I would be brave enough or generous enough to do that."

"And those trees in Trebah. Gosh, those enormous trees—what did they call them? 'champion trees?' Think about the people who planted those. It takes a lot of foresight to plant a tree, doesn't it?"

We talked about the hilarity of those mummers yesterday in Padstow with their boozy accordion band. Philip told a joke he'd read in the New Yorker, a cartoon actually: in the top half of the panel, the angel is greeting people at the gate of heaven with "Welcome to heaven; here's your harp." In the bottom panel, the devil is greeting people at the doorway to hell, saying "Welcome to hell; here's your accordion."

"Accordion music has gotten a lot better," I said. "It's not all Myron Floren and his *Disco Polka* album."

"You've just gotten a lot older," someone answered.

"OK, on that happy note, let's get out to the Firehouse before we lose our table." We headed down the Digey for the last time, turning right onto Fore Street. At the Firehouse, we went upstairs to the second floor where our table was waiting. Our view was of the harbor and Smeaton's Pier. We ordered a round of appetizers to share: salt & pepper squid with garlic mayonnaise, sticky belly pork & crispy crackling with an oriental sauce, and a bowl of mussels, just for old time's sake, Cornish mussels in a classic mariniere sauce.

We talked about seeing those silly grey—and gay—seals on Christmas Day and about how every single person standing on that cliff honored the need to be silent. We found it remarkable. Everyone respected the silence rule even though there were no signs, no instructions, and no one to keep order. "That's the way the world should work," someone said.

And we talked about the church service on Christmas morning. "What I liked," Claire started since she was our resident theologian, "was that the woman who preached made it all about life today instead of about some tale involving donkeys and sheep two thousand years ago. This idea she had, that we get it all wrong when we focus on the crib and the stable and all that, I really got what she meant. I wondered why they didn't have a creche. But her point, that if you just focus on that, you miss the meaning of this day. How did she say it?"

"I think it was that if you sing a Christmas carol and feel all nostalgic about it but fail to feed the hungry or help immigrants or come to the aid of people who are under attack, you aren't getting it. You don't understand Christmas. Her way of saying it was good. What Christmas proves is that the light is stronger than the darkness, even the darkness of hate and violence."

"Yeah. But she also said that this isn't about some baby from the first century. Remember that? It's about us. Doesn't sound very Jingle Bellsy, but I think she was right."

"And standing in front of Hepworth's *Madonna and Child* in the Lady Chapel really choked me up. She had children, too, and knows. She knows. The tender way that mother held her son will always stick with me. It was a picture of Hepworth's broken heart. Gosh, Barbara Hepworth. This was her town, wasn't it? I can't believe we met this giant of a woman who had such a genius for sculpture."

"I liked that the music was singable," Mark added. "I hate unsingable church music."

"I loved waking up to the smell of coffee and sausage that morning, Philip," I said. "You are old Mr. Badger, aren't you?"

"I guess I sorta am," he admitted. "I didn't know that until this week, though. I guess being the homemaker has made me this way."

"Well, do you have room for another homemaker, my dear?" Claire said, reaching for his hand across the table. "Because I'm there, too, now. I know I'm outta practice, but just you wait. I've got some tricks up my sleeve."

"Best news of the week," Philip said, smiling at her. "Welcome home, Honey. We'll get these guys over to supper in a couple of weeks and show 'em what we've learned here."

Philip went on. "We certainly made this our home. I feel tonight like I belong here somehow. The fisherman's cottage was perfect. We wandered all over Cornwall, but we always knew the road home, didn't we? I'm gonna miss this place."

The main courses came to the table, and they looked pretty darn good. You'd have thought none of us had eaten for the whole week. Claire had ordered the Thai seafood curry, which included a generous amount of local white fish, tiger prawns, and mussels. The minute I saw it, I had fish curry envy. Mark had the Newlyn cod—caught just a few miles from here near Penzance—served with hollandaise sauce and the first skinny fries we'd seen on the trip. We ordered a second plate of those salty fries, and all helped ourselves. Philip had the goat cheese pizza on a super-thin crust, with sun-dried tomatoes, black olives, red peppers, rocket pesto & mozzarella. The rocket pesto added a rich and fiery flavor. And finally—I just couldn't help myself—I had their steak and Guinness pie, just to be able to compare it with other steak pies I'd had that week. (They were all good.) It was loaded with local Cornish beef, gravy, and mushrooms—and topped with a pastry crown. Gorgeous.

Before we ate, we toasted the local farmers and fisher people, the shopkeepers of St Ives and the garden keepers of England. We toasted each other for being affable companions and laughing so easily. We toasted friends back home, the family we had missed, and the oven in the fisherman's cottage. "I'm sick of toasting that oven," Mark said. "I do think we have to let the owners know the damn thing only works once a week."

"But here's the deal," I threw in. "The damn thing worked for us. We have to toast that Christmas dinner, Mark. Gosh, what a lovely time. The beef, the veg, those remarkable, goose-fat-soaked potatoes. Oh my. The whole day was just perfect for us. And here's to that plucky old corkscrew, once we finally found it, *Claire*," I said, directing my emphasis to her. "And to you two clever Toads," I said to Claire and Philip, "for that dessert. Wow."

"Well, we owe that to Mary Berry."

And then we dug into our supper. We went quiet for a while as we took our first bites. We were all feeling a little reflective on this final evening in town. For the first time this week, except for that ride back from Godrevy on Christmas day, we were all silent.

"OK, favorites," Mark said, breaking the silence as he put down his fork and took a swallow of ale. "I think my favorite moment was all of us working in the kitchen on Christmas Day. Even you, Claire," he said, referring to the little food fight she started. "I think I understand now why you liked old Mr. Toad."

"That was not my fault. You had a very bop-able head. I think you were asking for it."

"Sounds like an abuser to me," he said. "Seriously, cooking together was a hoot. If someone had been recording the banter in that kitchen, we could all be in therapy on a group rate."

"Or in jail."

"And, by the way, as long as we're voting, I loved the Back-Street Bistro on Christmas Eve. Great choice, guys. I know you made that reservation in October to get us a table. Well done."

"We can't forget Ratty and Moley," Philip was proposing a toast. "I think they suited us so well because they spent all their time loafing, just like us. Or maybe we just didn't read about the work they had to do. I mean, they must have had to cut their firewood or carry in the provisions. Where did the Badger get all that ham and eggs he served up for breakfast that morning? Wait! What am I talking about? These are small forest and riverbank animals, not *people*. Anyway, here's to them, to their sweet way of taking care of each other and..."

"And what about Mr. Toad?" Claire loved that creature. "I'm sure he was a wounded child who was still working out his emotional distress…" she said, drifting off a bit. "Or am I talking about myself?" she said.

"I loved the Badger," I interrupted, "because this one here is *my badger*," I said, reaching out for Mark's hand. "Oh, honey, I used to think you were too kind to people, the way you took everyone in and the way you'd just talk with anyone, especially if they looked like they needed help. But now I see it. This is who *you* are, and I love you for it."

"My grandma Emma taught me that." He told us a wonderful story about how his maternal grandmother would come on the Greyhound Bus to visit in the Twin Cities, all the way from Mobridge, South Dakota. By the time the bus got to St Paul, she knew half the people on it and where they were headed. She reached out to them and showed interest in them, and it was very sincere. She had done the same for Mark. They were friends, and he took comfort in her care. Emma is very much a part of our lives now even though she's been meeting people in heaven since the 1980s.

"OK," Claire stepped in. "everyone, now be honest, whose small plate did you love the most after we got home from Truro that night? Mark's scallops, Philip's brisket, or my fish and chips?" No one wanted to start down that road. Philip took a forkful of pie. Mark took a long drink from his pint.

"Oh, honey," I finally said to Claire, "you're all cute. I never pick favorites."

"Yes, you do," Mark said. "You told me my *Coquilles* was the best."

"Oh well, maybe I did. But here's something: Do you remember putting a backpack on your head at Cape Cornwall, Claire? That was possibly the funniest moment of the week—except for the seagull that took a poop on Mark's head. I didn't dare laugh. That and the bag Philip used. Do you remember the look that young mom gave you? It was, like, 'Stay away from my kid!' They must have thought we were bonkers."

"It's OK to be bonkers."

"Oh gosh, my favorite moment," Philip said. "Let me think. I loved that first solo voice at Lessons and Carols. It was unforgettable. I still get goosebumps. And that table next to the fire over at Zennor. What was the name of that pub again?"

"The Tinners Arms."

"Yeah, that was it. With the dogs and the neighbors and the fire. I loved that place."

"Oh, and those wonderful, holy nuns," Claire said. "My favorite moment of the week for sure. I can't remember the name of that town or even the pub where we had lunch, but what a sensation it was to sit there in that chapel with those nuns praying away like mad, with all that candle wax and incense. I'll never forget it. I think at that moment I had a sort of calling; I don't know. I felt surrounded by warmth and love. It was completely unexpected and pretty amazing," she said. Philip reached out and touched her hand.

"What was it, do you think, Honey?"

"I don't know. It was a power of some kind, a force of absolute love. It might have been like Ratty and Moley when they met the Friend and Helper. Those women are pretty counter-cultural; in the good sense, I mean." She trailed off and was looking out the window at the harbor below. "It takes a lot of courage for them to take on the world the way they do," she finally said. "Here's to those ladies!"

"Do you know what we never did, you guys?" someone said. "We never went to the Tate. We said on our first day here that we'd do that, but it never happened. Oh well, it means we have to come back."

"And shoot, we forgot to do that art crawl through the Downalong. Here's to next year! Same place, same cottage, next year!" We all toasted, but we all knew it wouldn't happen.

"How about that long walk along the coast that first day? Remember the cliffs and hollows, with the wind rushing up and around us? I felt like it blew all the anxiety out of me, whatever that means. And to that crazy flock of sheep."

"And here's to Babs Hepworth," Philip offered, raising a glass which we all matched. "She was a piece of work, that one."

Had we finally run out of toasts? We indeed had finished our meal, and the check was on the table. As we'd been doing all week, we split the bill and paid up, but we felt like lingering this evening.

Since we'd eaten all the chocolate in our cottage, and Claire had polished off the last of the shortbread, we decided to share a couple of desserts. But instead of having them here at the Firehouse we decided it was still early enough to catch the dessert course at the Alba Restaurant just down the street. Over the years, Mark and I have had some truly memorable meals at the Alba. We hustled down the stairs of the Firehouse and dashed headlong out onto the street—and into a gale of rain!

"Let's run for it," we hollered, and down Fore Street we flew, scarves and jackets blowing in the wind. We dashed around the corner onto Life Boat Hill, down to the harbor, a sharp left, and into the door. Whew! We hurried upstairs to the dining room where we arrived just in time for late evening tables to have opened up. We dried off looking slightly crazed, and we were treated like we were royalty.

We shared two remarkable desserts. One was a lemon meringue with marinated strawberries. I'm not sure what it was in which they were marinated, but I didn't realize that a strawberry could be improved so much. The chef presented the meringue with vanilla Chantilly, which is a topping that involves pouring cream over vanilla beans and whipping it lightly with sugar until it's like velvet. On the side, he served strawberry sorbet, herbs, several variations of strawberry gel, and a tuille, which is a light, crisp wafer. Seeing us hover around the table, they brought us four tuilles. Very gracious.

So that was the lemon half. The second dessert was called "Chocolate Nemesis" and consisted of hot chocolate fondant with malted milk sorbet, chocolate syrup, and salted caramel drops with a delicious pastry shard. Every one of us groaned with pleasure at the first bite.

We shouldn't have done it, but we also ordered a half bottle of Elysium Black Muscat from the Andrew Quady winery which is in Madera, California. It paired perfectly with both desserts, and we toasted this as a fitting end to a week of shared meals. Tomorrow we would start the journey back to our real homes and leave St Ives and our temporary home at the fisherman's cottage behind.

As we sipped the final bit of that wine, one of us said, "You know what, you guys. No one toasted our house here tonight but wasn't that a lovely place to make our own? The whole place just seemed to suit us, not too big and not too small."

"A really spacious bathroom."

"I loved the kitchen."

"You gotta admit, we put in a lot of time in front of that fireplace, didn't we? It sorta made the house work."

"How about that Christmas dinner we had around that table? I'll always remember that."

Claire proposed the final toast. "To our quest this week for good food, love, and a corkscrew. To each other and the world. And to the fisherman's cottage."

Made in the USA
Lexington, KY
02 September 2019